Rhythm Mastery for Guitarists: Unlocking Tempo and Timing Techniques For Guitar Composition

University Scholastic Press

Copyright © 2024 by University Scholastic Press

No part of this publication may be reproduced, stored in a retrieval system, or transmitted in any form or by any means, electronic, mechanical, photocopying, recording, scanning, or otherwise, without the prior written permission of the author.

This publication is designed to provide accurate and authoritative information in regards to the subject matter covered. It is sold with the understanding that neither the author nor the publisher is engaged in rendering legal, investment, accounting, or other professional services.

While the author has used their best efforts in preparing this book, they make no representations or warranties with respect to the accuracy or completeness of the contents of this book and specifically disclaim any implied warranties of merchantability or fitness for a particular purpose. No warranty may be created or extended by sales representatives or written sales materials. The advice and strategies contained herein may not be suitable for your situation. You should consult with a professional when appropriate. The author shall be liable for any loss of profit or any other commercial damages, including but not limited to special, incidental, consequential, personal, or other damages.

Other Musician's Series Books
By University Scholastic Press:

A Guitarist's Grimoire: Unlocking the Secrets of Creating A Musical Diary To Master Guitar Composition

Storytelling With Sound: Fundamentals of Creative Guitar Composition

Musical Architecture Secrets: Structure Planning For Guitar Composition

Strings Of Brilliance: Mastering Melody and Harmony Development For Guitar Composition

Rhythm Mastery for Guitarists: Unlocking Tempo and Timing Techniques For Guitar Composition

Table Of Contents

INTRODUCTION

Welcome to *Rhythm Mastery for Guitarists: Unlocking Tempo and Timing Techniques For Guitar Composition.* Whether you're a seasoned musician looking to deepen your understanding of rhythm or a novice eager to explore the rhythmic landscape of guitar composition, this comprehensive guide is designed to be your trusted companion on the journey toward rhythmic proficiency.

In the world of music, rhythm is the heartbeat that drives every composition, infusing it with energy, emotion, and character. For guitarists, mastering rhythm unlocks the door to endless creative possibilities, allowing you to craft compositions that resonate deeply with your audience. This book is crafted to empower you with the knowledge and skills necessary to become a master of rhythm, guiding you through every aspect of tempo, timing, and rhythmic technique with clarity and precision.

Each chapter of this book is meticulously structured to provide a thorough exploration of various rhythmic concepts and their application to guitar composition. From understanding the fundamental principles of rhythmic patterns and timing to delving into advanced topics such as polyrhythms, syncopation, and tempo changes, you will embark on a comprehensive journey that will elevate your rhythmic prowess to new heights.

One of the unique features of this book is the inclusion of rhythm maps, which serve as invaluable tools for your compositional journey. These maps offer visual representations of rhythmic structures, helping you to organize and conceptualize your compositions with clarity and coherence. Whether you're mapping out strumming patterns, exploring complex time signatures, or experimenting with tempo changes, these maps will serve as your navigational guide through the rhythmic landscape.

As you progress through the chapters of this book, you'll not only develop a deeper understanding of rhythm but also cultivate your own unique rhythmic voice as a guitarist. Whether you're drawing inspiration from diverse musical genres, collaborating with other musicians, or honing your technical skills, you'll discover a wealth of practical strategies and insights to enhance your rhythmic creativity.

Above all, remember that mastery of rhythm is a journey, not a destination. Embrace the process, stay curious, and allow yourself the freedom to explore and experiment. With dedication, patience, and a spirit of adventure, you will unlock the full potential of rhythm and unleash your creativity as a guitarist.

So, without further ado, let's embark on this rhythmic odyssey together. The stage is set, the rhythm awaits – let's dive in and begin our journey toward rhythm mastery.

RHYTHMIC PATTERNS AND TIMING

Rhythms provide structure, drive, and energy, shaping the overall feel of your composition.

CREATING RHYTHMIC PATTERNS FOR SECTIONS

Creating rhythmic patterns for each section in your guitar composition is a fundamental aspect of crafting a dynamic and engaging piece of music.

We'll learn in this chapter how to create rhythmic patterns for different sections in your guitar composition. But first, we have some questions to gain greater clarity.

UNDERSTAND THE OVERALL FEEL

Before diving into specific rhythmic patterns, have a clear understanding of the overall feel or mood you want to convey in each section. The rhythmic character should align with the emotional content of the music.

When aiming to have a clear understanding of the overall feel or mood you want to convey in each section of your guitar composition, asking yourself thoughtful questions can guide your creative process.

What Emotion Am I Conveying?

Question: What specific emotion or combination of emotions do I want the audience to feel in this section?

How Does This Section Fit into the Overall Narrative?

Question: What role does this section play in the larger narrative or structure of my composition?

What Imagery or Story Does the Section Evoke?

Question: If my composition were to tell a story, what imagery or narrative does this section evoke?

Which Key or Mode Best Represents the Desired Mood?

Question: Have I chosen the right key or mode that aligns with the emotional tone I want for this section?

Are There Specific Chord Progressions That Convey the Mood?

Question: How can I use chord progressions to enhance the emotional impact of this section?

What Dynamics Will Best Convey the Intended Feel?

Question: Should this section be loud and powerful, soft and delicate, or somewhere in between?

Are There Specific Guitar Techniques That Enhance the Mood?

Question: How can I utilize techniques like slides, bends, vibrato, or fingerpicking to enhance the emotional quality?

Does the Tempo Reflect the Intended Atmosphere?

Question: Is the tempo appropriate for the mood I want to create, or should I consider changes in tempo?

How Will Rhythm Contribute to the Overall Feel?

Question: What rhythmic patterns can contribute to the desired atmosphere? Should I experiment with syncopation or steady beats?

What Is the Role of Melody in Conveying Emotion?

Question: How can the melody in this section contribute to the emotional impact? Are there specific intervals or motifs that evoke the desired mood?

Is There a Contrast Between This Section and Previous Ones?

Question: How does the mood in this section contrast or complement the moods in the sections that precede and follow it?

Are There Specific Influences or Inspirations for This Section?

Question: Are there musical or non-musical influences that inspire the mood I want to achieve in this section?

Should I Consider Textures and Timbres to Enhance the Feel?

Question: How can the choice of textures and timbres contribute to the overall feel? Should I explore different voicings or tonal qualities?

Does the Section Serve a Transitional Purpose in the Composition?

Question: If this section serves as a transition, how can I use that transition to affect the mood dynamically?

How Can I Engage the Listener Emotionally?

Question: What elements can I incorporate to engage the listener emotionally and make this section memorable?

What Do I Want the Listener to Take Away from This Section?

Question: What impression or emotional residue do I want this section to leave on the listener?

Have I Listened to the Section Objectively to Assess Its Mood?

Question: Am I actively listening to the section, putting myself in the shoes of the audience to evaluate the conveyed mood?

By asking yourself these questions, you can gain a deeper understanding of the emotions and atmospheres you want to convey in each section of your guitar composition. This self-inquiry will guide your creative decisions and lead to a more intentional and evocative musical experience for your audience.

TEMPO AND TIME SIGNATURE

Set the tempo and time signature for your composition. These elements serve as the foundation for creating rhythmic patterns and will influence the overall pacing of the music.

DEFINING TEMPO AND TIME SIGNATURE

Setting the tempo and time signature for your guitar composition is a crucial step that establishes the rhythmic foundation of your music. These elements significantly influence the overall feel and structure of your composition.

SETTING THE TEMPO

Identify the Mood and Style:
Consider the mood and style of your composition. Faster tempos often convey excitement or urgency, while slower tempos evoke a more contemplative or relaxed atmosphere.

Experiment with Different Tempos:
Play through sections of your composition at various tempos to find the one that best suits the emotional tone you want to convey.

Consider Technical Demands:
Take into account the technical demands of your composition. A faster tempo might add complexity, so ensure it aligns with the playability of the guitar parts.

Common Tempos and Their Associations:

- Allegro (Fast): 120-168 BPM - Energetic, lively.
- Moderato (Moderate): 108-120 BPM - Moderate pace.
- Andante (Walking Pace): 76-108 BPM - Flowing and expressive.
- Adagio (Slow): 66-76 BPM - Slow and stately.

Examples:

- If your composition is an upbeat and energetic piece, a **tempo** around **140 BPM** might work well.
- For a contemplative and expressive ballad, a **tempo** around **80 BPM** could be suitable.

SETTING THE TIME SIGNATURE

Determine the Feel and Accentuation:

Decide on the feel of your composition—whether it's a straightforward pulse or has a more complex, syncopated rhythm.

Experiment with Different Time Signatures:

Try out various time signatures to see how they affect the rhythmic flow. Common time signatures for guitar include 4/4, 3/4, 6/8, and 12/8.

Match Time Signature to Phrasing:

Match the time signature to the natural phrasing of your melodies and chords. Some compositions may naturally fit a 3/4 waltz feel, while others may suit the more standard 4/4 time.

Consider Genre Conventions:

Be aware of genre conventions. For instance, many rock and pop songs use 4/4, while certain Latin styles may incorporate 3/4 or 6/8.

Examples:

- If your composition has a driving and straightforward feel, **4/4** could be appropriate.
- For a waltz-like composition, **3/4** might enhance the flowing and dance-like quality.

COMBINING TEMPO AND TIME SIGNATURE

Synergy between Tempo and Time Signature:

Ensure that the chosen tempo and time signature complement each other, creating a cohesive rhythmic structure.

Adaptation for Different Sections:

Consider adapting the tempo or time signature for different sections of your composition to add variety and interest.

Transitional Considerations:

Pay attention to transitions between sections. Gradual tempo changes or time signature shifts can create dynamic contrast.

Examples:

In a composition with a fast and energetic introduction, starting in **4/4 at 150 BPM** could set an invigorating tone.

Transitioning to a slower section in **3/4 at 80 BPM** could introduce a contrasting and reflective mood.

Remember, these are guidelines, and there's room for creativity. Experimenting with different tempos and time signatures can lead to unexpected and exciting results. Trust your musical instincts and choose elements that best serve the emotional expression and character of your guitar composition.

KEY RHYTHMIC ELEMENTS

Identify key rhythmic elements in each section, such as accents, syncopations, and subdivisions. These elements contribute to the groove and character of the rhythm.

IDENTIFY RHYTHMIC ELEMENTS

Identifying key rhythmic elements in each section of your guitar composition is essential for creating a dynamic and engaging musical experience. Rhythm serves as the heartbeat of your piece, shaping its character and providing a sense of movement.

Understand the Basic Rhythmic Structure:

Listening Tip: Play through the section and identify the primary rhythmic pattern that underlies the melody and chords.

ACCENTS

Identify Accentuated Beats:

Listening Tip: Listen for beats that are emphasized or stand out compared to others.

Experiment with Different Accent Patterns:

Example: In a 4/4 time signature, experiment with accents on the 2nd and 4th beats for a backbeat feel commonly found in rock and pop.

Identify Offbeat Rhythms:

Listening Tip: Pay attention to moments where notes are played on offbeats or between the main beats.

Create Syncopated Patterns:

Example: Instead of playing a chord on the downbeat, try strumming on the "and" of a beat to introduce syncopation and energy.

SUBDIVISIONS

Determine Subdivision Patterns:

Listening Tip: Analyze how each beat is subdivided (e.g., eighth notes, sixteenth notes) to uncover intricate rhythms.

Experiment with Varied Subdivisions:

Example: If the section primarily uses eighth notes, experiment with introducing sixteenth-note patterns to add complexity and excitement.

Polyrhythms and Cross-Rhythms:

Listening Tip: Explore instances where different rhythmic patterns overlap, creating polyrhythmic or cross-rhythmic effects.

Example: Overlapping a 3/4 pattern with a 4/4 pattern can create interesting polyrhythmic textures, adding depth to your composition.

Tempo Changes:

Listening Tip: Consider whether the section would benefit from tempo changes to alter the mood or intensity.

Example: Gradually increasing the tempo in a build-up section can add tension and anticipation.

Drum Patterns as Inspiration:

Listening Tip: Listen to drum patterns in various genres for inspiration on incorporating rhythmic elements.

Example: Incorporate a percussive strumming pattern inspired by drum patterns used in funk or Latin music.

Dynamic Rhythmic Contrast:

Listening Tip: Identify sections where you want to introduce dynamic contrast by changing the rhythmic feel.

Example: Contrast a legato, flowing section with a staccato, punctuated section for variety.

Silences and Rests:

Listening Tip: Pay attention to moments of silence or rests, as they are integral to the rhythmic structure.

Example: Introduce brief silences between phrases to create rhythmic tension and anticipation.

Recording and Analyzing:

Listening Tip: Record yourself playing the section and listen critically to identify subtle rhythmic nuances.

Example: Use recording software or apps to visualize the waveform and pinpoint specific rhythmic elements.

Collaborative Rhythmic Exploration:

Listening Tip: If collaborating with others, encourage exploration of rhythmic ideas during jam sessions or rehearsals.

Example: Collaborators can contribute unique rhythmic elements, enhancing the overall complexity and depth of your composition.

By actively listening, experimenting, and being mindful of various rhythmic elements, you can craft sections that are rhythmically engaging and align with the emotional and stylistic goals of your guitar composition. Always trust your instincts and allow your creativity to guide your exploration of rhythmic possibilities.

RHYTHMIC MOTIF

Create a rhythmic motif or theme that serves as a unifying element throughout a section. This motif can be a short rhythmic pattern that repeats, providing coherence and structure.

ESTABLISH A RHYTHMIC MOTIF

Establishing a rhythmic motif is a powerful way to create coherence and a distinctive identity for your guitar composition. A rhythmic motif serves as a recurring rhythmic pattern or theme that ties different sections of your composition together.

Below we'll learn how to establish a rhythmic motif for your guitar composition.

Identify Key Rhythmic Elements:

Listening Tip: Play through the composition and identify recurring rhythmic elements that naturally stand out or create a sense of identity.

Focus on Signature Patterns:

Listening Tip: Identify any unique rhythmic patterns that can be considered the signature of a particular section.

Isolate a Core Rhythmic Idea:

Listening Tip: Isolate a short rhythmic phrase that captures the essence of a section.

EXPERIMENT WITH VARIATIONS

Subdivisions:

Example: If your core rhythmic idea involves eighth notes, experiment with variations using sixteenth notes or triplets.

Dynamics:

Example: Play with dynamic contrasts within the motif—perhaps emphasizing certain beats or strums.

Rests and Silences:

Example: Introduce pauses or rests within the motif for added rhythmic interest.

Adapt Motif to Different Sections:

Listening Tip: Consider how the rhythmic motif can be adapted to suit the mood and dynamics of different sections.

Example: A subdued, introspective section may use a simplified version of the motif, while an energetic section may feature an embellished variation.

Incorporate Syncopation or Offbeat Elements:

Listening Tip: Experiment with syncopated rhythms or offbeat accents to add rhythmic complexity.

Example: If your motif involves strumming on the downbeat, try accentuating offbeats for a syncopated feel.

Drum and Percussion Inspiration:

Listening Tip: Draw inspiration from drum patterns or percussion elements in various genres to infuse rhythmic creativity.

Example: If your motif lacks percussive elements, consider incorporating a percussive strumming technique or tapping on the guitar body.

Consider Tempo Changes:

Listening Tip: Evaluate whether the rhythmic motif can adapt to gradual tempo changes for added dynamics.

Example: A motif played at a faster tempo during an intense section can convey a sense of urgency.

Recording and Analyzing:

Listening Tip: Record yourself playing the motif and listen critically to identify nuances and potential refinements.

Example: Use recording software to visualize the waveform, ensuring consistency in the motif's rhythmic structure.

Collaborative Exploration:

Listening Tip: If collaborating with other musicians, encourage them to explore variations or contribute ideas to enhance the rhythmic motif.

Example: Collaborators can add percussion, additional rhythmic layers, or suggest modifications that elevate the motif.

Evaluate for Consistency:

Listening Tip: Ensure that the rhythmic motif maintains a level of consistency while allowing for appropriate variations.

Example: Consistency in the motif's core elements helps create a recognizable and memorable rhythmic identity.

Rhythmic Call and Response:

Listening Tip: Explore call-and-response dynamics within the motif, creating conversational rhythmic phrases.

Example: One guitar part introduces a rhythmic idea, and another guitar part responds with a complementary rhythm.

Refinement and Finalization:

Listening Tip: Refine the rhythmic motif based on your critical analysis and finalize it as a distinctive rhythmic theme.

Example: Ensure that the motif aligns with the overall mood and intention of your composition.

By carefully crafting and developing a rhythmic motif, you create a rhythmic backbone that unifies your composition and provides a recognizable theme for your listeners. Regularly revisit and refine the motif as your composition evolves, ensuring that it remains a cohesive and integral part of the musical narrative.

RHYTHMIC DENSITY

Vary the rhythmic density within each section. Experiment with passages of dense, intricate rhythms followed by moments of simplicity. This variation adds interest and dynamic contrast.

VARY RHYTHMIC DENSITY

Varying rhythmic density within each section of your guitar composition is a dynamic way to engage your audience and create interest. Rhythmic density refers to the quantity and distribution of rhythmic elements within a given timeframe.

We dive into how to effectively vary rhythmic density and keep your composition engaging below.

Identify the Primary Rhythmic Density:

Listening Tip: Play through the section and identify the predominant rhythmic density, which might involve consistent patterns or sustained notes.

Choose Moments for Variation:

Listening Tip: Pinpoint sections or moments in your composition where a change in rhythmic density could enhance the musical narrative.

EXPLORE CHANGES IN SUBDIVISIONS

Increase Subdivisions:

Example: If your primary rhythmic density involves quarter notes, try increasing the subdivisions to eighth notes or sixteenth notes for a busier texture.

Decrease Subdivisions:

Example: Conversely, simplify a dense rhythmic pattern by reducing subdivisions, creating a more spacious feel.

Dynamic Contrasts:

Listening Tip: Consider how dynamic changes can affect rhythmic density. Louder, more intense moments often benefit from increased density.

Example: During a climactic section, intensify the rhythmic density by incorporating rapid strumming or picking patterns.

Incorporate Syncopation and Offbeats:

Listening Tip: Experiment with syncopated rhythms or placing accents on offbeats to add complexity without necessarily increasing the number of notes.

Example: Introduce syncopation by accentuating offbeats within a primarily straightforward rhythm.

Utilize Rests and Silences:

Listening Tip: Introduce moments of rest or silence strategically to create rhythmic contrast and emphasize specific beats.

Example: Pause between phrases or chord changes to create a rhythmic "breath" in the music.

EXPLORE RHYTHMIC PATTERNS

Switch Between Patterns:

Example: Alternate between different rhythmic patterns, providing variation and maintaining the listener's interest.

Cross-Rhythms:

Example: Experiment with cross-rhythms where different instruments or hands play contrasting rhythmic patterns simultaneously.

Gradual Buildups and Decreases:

Listening Tip: Use gradual changes in rhythmic density to build tension or create a sense of release.

Example: Begin a section with sparse, isolated notes and gradually build up to a denser, more intricate pattern.

Dynamic Layering:

Listening Tip: Layer different rhythmic elements on top of each other to create a textured, multidimensional sound.

Example: Combine arpeggios, strumming, and percussion-like techniques to layer rhythmic complexity.

Contrast Sections with Different Densities:

Listening Tip: Consider having sections with distinct rhythmic densities to delineate different moods or transitions.

Example: Transition from a sparse, introspective verse to a lively, rhythmically dense chorus.

Explore Drum and Percussive Techniques:

Listening Tip: Incorporate drumming and percussion-inspired techniques to enhance rhythmic complexity.

Example: Use techniques like palm muting, tapping, or percussive strumming to add percussive elements to your playing.

Experiment with Tempo Changes:

Listening Tip: Explore how tempo changes can influence the perception of rhythmic density.

Example: Increase the tempo during a section to create a sense of urgency and higher rhythmic density.

Collaborative Exploration:

Listening Tip: If collaborating with other musicians, encourage rhythmic experimentation during jam sessions or rehearsals.

Example: Collaborators can contribute ideas for rhythmic variation, leading to unexpected and exciting changes in density.

Evaluate Consistency:

Listening Tip: Ensure that variations in rhythmic density serve the overall musical narrative and maintain a sense of cohesion.

Example: While variations are crucial, consistency is key to avoid creating a disjointed or chaotic feel.

Intentionally varying rhythmic density within each section, adds depth and excitement. These changes create a sense of ebb and flow, keeping your audience engaged and enhancing the overall musical experience. Trust your creative instincts, experiment with different rhythmic approaches, and enjoy the process of sculpting the rhythmic landscape of your composition.

SUBDIVISIONS

Experiment with different rhythmic subdivisions, such as eighth notes, sixteenth notes, triplets, or other subdivisions that suit the style of your composition. Mixing subdivisions adds rhythmic diversity.

EXPERIMENTING WITH SUBDIVISIONS

Rhythmic subdivisions are the way musical time is divided into smaller, equal parts. Experimenting with different rhythmic subdivisions in your guitar composition can greatly influence its feel, adding variety and interest.

UNDERSTANDING RHYTHMIC SUBDIVISIONS

Basic Subdivisions:
In most music, the fundamental subdivision is typically into two parts per beat, creating a binary or duple feel (e.g., quarter notes in 4/4 time). This creates a straightforward, even-paced rhythm.

Variety of Subdivisions:
However, music can be divided into a variety of subdivisions, such as eighth notes, triplets, sixteenth notes, quintuplets, and beyond. Each subdivision brings its own rhythmic flavor and complexity.

Syncopation and Offbeats:
Rhythmic subdivisions play a crucial role in creating syncopation by placing accents on offbeats. This adds complexity and can make the rhythm more interesting and dynamic.

DIFFERENT RHYTHMIC SUBDIVISIONS

Basic Eighth Note Subdivision:

Example: If your composition primarily uses quarter notes, experiment with incorporating eighth notes to add a sense of movement.

Triplet Subdivision:

Example: Transform a straight rhythm by using triplets. In 4/4 time, three eighth-note triplets span one quarter note, creating a unique feel.

Sixteenth Note Subdivision:

Example: Enhance rhythmic complexity by introducing sixteenth notes. This subdivision allows for intricate patterns and faster-paced rhythms.

Dotted Rhythms:

Example: Use dotted rhythms, where a note is extended by half its value. For instance, a dotted eighth note followed by a sixteenth note can create a distinctive, swinging feel.

Quintuplets and Septuplets:

Example: Experiment with less common subdivisions like quintuplets (5 notes per beat) or septuplets (7 notes per beat) for a more complex and unexpected rhythmic texture.

Changing Subdivisions Across Sections:

Example: Shift between subdivisions in different sections to create contrast. Start with a simple subdivision and gradually introduce more complex ones.

Polyrhythms:

Example: Introduce polyrhythms by overlaying different subdivisions simultaneously. For example, play triplets on one hand while playing sixteenth notes on the other.

Accented Offbeats:

Example: Accent offbeats within a subdivision to create syncopation. For instance, emphasize the "and" in eighth-note subdivisions.

Syncopated Patterns:

Example: Create syncopated patterns by placing accents on unexpected beats or subdivisions within a measure.

Cross-Rhythms:

Example: Play different subdivisions in different instruments or hands, creating cross-rhythms. This can add depth and complexity to your composition.

Dynamic Changes in Subdivisions:

Example: Gradually change the subdivision density throughout a section. Start with sparse subdivisions and gradually increase the complexity.

Emulate Percussion Techniques:

Example: Emulate percussive techniques by using subdivisions to mimic drum patterns. Explore techniques like rim clicks or muted strumming for rhythmic variety.

Combining Subdivisions:

Example: Combine different subdivisions within a phrase or lick to create intricate and evolving rhythmic patterns.

Interplay with Melody:

Example: Coordinate rhythmic subdivisions with melodic elements, ensuring a seamless interplay that enhances the overall musical expression.

Utilize Rests:

Example: Introduce rests within subdivisions strategically. A well-placed rest can create rhythmic tension and contribute to the overall feel of a passage.

Collaborative Exploration:

Example: If collaborating with other musicians, encourage experimentation with various subdivisions during jam sessions or rehearsals.

Record and Analyze:

Example: Record your playing to analyze how different subdivisions contribute to the overall feel. Listen critically to identify patterns that work well or need adjustment.

Experimenting with rhythmic subdivisions not only enhances the complexity of your composition but also provides a platform for creative expression. Be open to trying new rhythmic ideas, and let the experimentation process guide you to unique and captivating rhythmic elements within your guitar composition.

SYNCOPATION

Introduce syncopated rhythms to enhance the groove of your composition. Syncopation involves emphasizing offbeat or unexpected accents, creating a sense of forward momentum.

USING SYNCOPATION FOR GROOVE

Introducing syncopated rhythms is an excellent way to enhance the groove and rhythmic interest in your guitar composition. Syncopation involves placing accents on offbeats or weak parts of the beat, creating a sense of surprise and movement.

Understand the Basics of Syncopation:

Definition: Syncopation involves emphasizing weak beats, offbeats, or the spaces between beats, creating an unexpected and dynamic feel.

Identify Target Offbeats:

Listening Tip: Identify specific offbeats or weak beats where you want to introduce syncopation within your composition.

Experiment with Basic Syncopation:

Example: Instead of playing a chord on the downbeat, try strumming or picking on the "and" of the beat, creating a simple yet effective syncopated rhythm.

Syncopated Strumming Patterns:

Example: Use a syncopated strumming pattern by accentuating the upstrokes. For instance, emphasize the "and" when strumming eighth notes.

Palm Muting for Syncopation:

Example: Apply palm muting to certain offbeats or weak beats to create a percussive, syncopated effect. This works well for adding groove to funky or rock-inspired compositions.

Accentuating Ties and Slurs:

Example: Accentuate tied or slurred notes across the bar line, creating a flowing, syncopated feel. This technique is effective in jazz and Latin-influenced styles.

Syncopated Arpeggios:

Example: Play arpeggios with a syncopated feel by accenting non-chord tones or picking specific notes on offbeats. This adds flair to arpeggio passages.

Syncopated Chord Progressions:

Example: Use syncopation in chord progressions by emphasizing specific chords on offbeats. This can create a rhythmic tension leading to the next section.

Cross-Rhythms for Advanced Syncopation:

Example: Experiment with cross-rhythms by playing different rhythmic patterns simultaneously. For instance, play triplets on one hand and eighth notes on the other.

Syncopated Bass Note Accents:

Example: Accentuate specific bass notes on offbeats, creating a syncopated foundation for the rest of the composition. This is effective in solo guitar arrangements.

Syncopated Riffs and Licks:

Example: Incorporate syncopation into memorable riffs or melodic licks. Accent certain notes on offbeats to add rhythmic interest.

Silences and Staccato for Emphasis:

Example: Introduce silences or staccato playing on offbeats to emphasize the syncopation. This technique is effective in funk and reggae genres.

Syncopated Percussive Techniques:

Example: Use percussive techniques, such as tapping or slapping the guitar body, on offbeats to enhance the overall rhythmic groove.

Cross-Hand Syncopation:

Example: Create syncopation by playing certain notes with one hand while muting or staccato striking the strings with the other hand. This adds complexity to fingerstyle playing.

Gradual Syncopation Buildups:

Example: Gradually introduce syncopation throughout a section, starting with simple rhythms and progressively adding more complex syncopated elements.

Syncopated Chordal Embellishments:

Example: Embellish chords with syncopated hammer-ons, pull-offs, or slides on specific offbeats. This technique adds flavor to chord progressions.

Explore Syncopation Across Genres:

Example: Experiment with syncopated rhythms in various genres, such as blues, jazz, funk, or Latin music. Each genre offers unique opportunities for syncopated expression.

Recording and Adjusting:

Listening Tip: Record your playing to assess how syncopation integrates into your composition. Make adjustments to the placement of accents for optimal groove.

Collaborate for Syncopated Ideas:

Listening Tip: If collaborating with other musicians, encourage them to contribute syncopated ideas during jam sessions or rehearsals.

Syncopation adds a sense of vitality and groove to your guitar composition. By experimenting with different syncopated techniques, you can elevate the rhythmic feel of your music and create an engaging and dynamic listening experience. Trust your musical instincts, explore various syncopated elements, and enjoy the process of infusing your composition with rhythmic energy.

STRUMMING PATTERNS

If your composition involves strummed chords, develop strumming patterns that complement the rhythmic feel. Strumming can add a percussive quality to the rhythm.

INCORPORATE STRUMMING PATTERNS

Incorporating diverse strumming patterns into your guitar composition is an excellent way to create distinct rhythmic patterns for each section, adding depth and dynamics to your music.

Downstrokes and Upstrokes:

Basic Pattern: Start with a simple downstroke and upstroke pattern. For example, down, down-up, down, up.

Application: Ideal for straightforward, driving rhythms. It suits sections with a steady, energetic feel.

Dotted Eighth-Note Pattern:

Basic Pattern: Emphasize the downbeat and the "and" of the beat, creating a dotted eighth-note feel. For example, down, down-up, down, down-up.

Application: Great for a subtle, swinging feel. Works well in folk, blues, or acoustic pop.

Sixteenth-Note Strumming:

Basic Pattern: Incorporate sixteenth notes for a faster-paced strumming pattern. For example, down-up-down-up.

Application: Useful in upbeat and lively sections. Ideal for pop, rock, or funk compositions.

Upstroke Emphasis:

Basic Pattern: Place emphasis on the upstrokes for a unique feel. For example, up, down, up, down.

Application: Adds a light and bouncy quality to the rhythm. Suitable for sections requiring a lighter touch.

Palm Muting Strumming:

Basic Pattern: Combine palm muting with a standard downstroke and upstroke pattern for a percussive effect. For example, palm mute down, palm mute up.

Application: Creates a rhythmic punch, often used in rock, metal, or funk compositions.

Fingerstyle Strumming:

Basic Pattern: Use fingerstyle techniques for a nuanced strumming pattern. For example, thumb, index, middle, ring.

Application: Perfect for sections requiring a softer, intricate touch. Well-suited for folk, classical, or acoustic genres.

Reggae-Style Strumming:

Basic Pattern: Incorporate a swung feel with a rhythmic accent on the third beat. For example, down, down-up, up.

Application: Evokes a laid-back, island vibe. Ideal for reggae, ska, or tropical-flavored compositions.

Flamenco-Style Rasgueado:

Basic Pattern: Use flamenco-inspired rasgueado strumming for a rapid, percussive effect. For example, outward rake, downward strum.

Application: Adds a dramatic and passionate flair. Well-suited for flamenco, Latin, or world music influences.

Arpeggio Strumming:

Basic Pattern: Break chords into individual arpeggios, strumming each note individually. For example, down, up, down, up.

Application: Creates a more delicate and intricate texture. Effective in sections requiring a softer touch or for highlighting individual notes within a chord progression.

Dynamic Strumming Variations:

Basic Pattern: Incorporate dynamic variations in strumming intensity and volume throughout a section.

Application: Adds emotional depth and expression. Suitable for sections where the intensity of the composition varies.

Muted Strumming Patterns:

Basic Pattern: Use muted strumming by placing the palm lightly on the strings while strumming. For example, muted down, muted up.

Application: Creates a percussive, rhythmic effect. Works well in funk, rock, or sections requiring a staccato feel.

Cross-Rhythmic Strumming:

Basic Pattern: Experiment with cross-rhythms, playing different strumming patterns simultaneously on different strings.

Application: Adds complexity and interest. Effective in creating intricate rhythmic patterns within a section.

Upbeat Chord Strumming:

Basic Pattern: Emphasize the upbeats while strumming chords, creating a lively and upbeat feel. For example, up, down-up, up, down-up.

Application: Ideal for uplifting sections or choruses. Suitable for pop, rock, or indie compositions.

Mixing Patterns for Sections:

Application: Combine different strumming patterns for various sections of your composition. For example, use a straightforward pattern for verses and a more complex one for the chorus.

Application: Adds dynamic contrast and keeps the listener engaged throughout the composition.

Funky Chord Scratching:

Basic Pattern: Create a percussive, staccato effect by scratching the strings with muted strums. For example, scratch, scratch, up, scratch.

Application: Ideal for funk and R&B-inspired sections, adding a rhythmic and funky groove.

Rhythmic Fingerstyle Patterns:

Basic Pattern: Explore intricate fingerstyle patterns for a melodic and rhythmic combination. For example, thumb, index, middle, thumb.

Application: Suitable for sections requiring a delicate and sophisticated rhythmic feel.

Jazz-Inspired Comping:

Basic Pattern: Use jazz-inspired comping with extended chords and syncopated strumming. For example, down-up, up, down-up.

Application: Perfect for jazz-influenced sections, providing a sophisticated and harmonically rich texture.

Slide Guitar Strumming:

Basic Pattern: Experiment with slide guitar techniques, sliding between chords while maintaining a rhythmic strumming pattern.

Application: Adds a bluesy or country feel, creating a distinctive and expressive sound.

Recording and Adjusting:

Listening Tip: Record your playing to assess how different strumming patterns integrate into your composition. Make adjustments to enhance groove and cohesion.

Collaborate for Strumming Ideas:

Listening Tip: If collaborating with other musicians, encourage them to contribute unique strumming ideas during jam sessions or rehearsals.

Incorporating a variety of strumming patterns into your guitar composition not only enhances the rhythm but also allows you to express different emotions and genres within your music. Experiment with these patterns, adapting them to suit the mood and dynamics of each section, and enjoy the creative process of crafting a rhythmic landscape for your composition.

PICKING PATTERNS

For fingerstyle or picked passages, experiment with different picking patterns. Varying the picking approach can create a wide range of rhythmic textures.

EXPERIMENTING WITH PICKING PATTERNS

Exploring various picking patterns is a fantastic way to add rhythmic diversity and enhance the overall texture of your guitar composition. Different picking techniques can provide unique tones and dynamics, contributing to the rhythmic timing of each section.

Let's explore various picking patterns, how to use them for rhythmic timing, and how to experiment with different patterns.

Alternate Picking:

Technique: Down-up motion, alternating between downstrokes and upstrokes.

Application: Versatile for various genres, providing a balanced and even attack.

Example: Apply alternate picking to scales, arpeggios, or melodic lines.

Economy Picking:

Technique: Minimizing motion by combining consecutive upstrokes or downstrokes.

Application: Efficient for rapid passages, particularly in jazz and shred guitar playing.

Example: Use economy picking for smooth execution of scalar runs or fast licks.

Hybrid Picking:

Technique: Combining pick and fingers for a hybrid approach.

Application: Ideal for creating a nuanced and dynamic sound, especially in country and fingerstyle genres.

Example: Use the pick for strings 1-4 and fingers for strings 5-6, creating a unique texture.

Fingerstyle Picking:

Technique: Using fingers (thumb, index, middle, ring) for picking instead of a pick.

Application: Great for intricate and melodic playing, common in classical and folk genres.

Example: Fingerpick chord progressions or intricate melodies.

Sweep Picking:

Technique: Employing a continuous motion in the same direction for consecutive notes on adjacent strings.

Application: Ideal for arpeggios and creating a smooth, flowing sound.

Example: Apply sweep picking to arpeggios for a cascading effect.

Tremolo Picking:

Technique: Rapidly picking a single note with a consistent, fast motion.

Application: Adds intensity and energy, often used in metal and classical compositions.

Example: Use tremolo picking for sustained notes or to build tension.

Chicken Pickin':

Technique: A percussive and staccato picking style, often associated with country music.

Application: Provides a sharp, snappy sound suitable for country and funk genres.

Example: Experiment with chicken pickin' on double stops or muted strings for a twangy effect.

Pinch Harmonics:

Technique: Simultaneously picking and lightly touching the string with the thumb to create harmonic overtones.

Application: Adds a squealing, edgy sound, commonly used in rock and metal.

Example: Apply pinch harmonics during lead guitar phrases for expressive accents.

Flatpicking:

Technique: Holding the pick firmly and using a flat edge for a clean and precise attack.

Application: Common in bluegrass and folk, offering clarity in fast-paced passages.

Example: Use flatpicking for rapid runs or melodic lines in acoustic compositions.

Combining Picking Styles:

Application: Experiment with switching between picking styles within a section for dynamic contrast.

Example: Combine fingerstyle picking with flatpicking for a versatile sound palette.

Staccato Picking:

Technique: Emphasizing short, disconnected notes by releasing pressure on the fretting hand.

Application: Adds a percussive quality, suitable for funk, reggae, or rhythmic emphasis.

Example: Apply staccato picking to emphasize rhythmic accents within chord progressions.

Crosspicking:

Technique: A combination of alternate picking and flatpicking, creating a rolling, arpeggiated effect.

Application: Ideal for intricate patterns and melodic embellishments.

Example: Use crosspicking to navigate through complex chord progressions.

Dynamic Picking:

Application: Experiment with varying picking intensity and dynamics to create expressive phrases.

Example: Play a melody softly and gradually increase picking intensity during a crescendo.

Syncopated Picking Patterns:

Technique: Introduce syncopated patterns by emphasizing offbeats or syncopated accents.

Application: Adds groove and rhythm to chord progressions or melodic lines.

Example: Accentuate offbeats with downstrokes or upstrokes for a syncopated feel.

Recording and Adjusting:

Listening Tip: Record your playing to analyze how different picking patterns integrate into your composition. Make adjustments to achieve optimal rhythmic timing.

Collaborate for Picking Ideas:

Listening Tip: If collaborating with other musicians, encourage them to contribute unique picking ideas during jam sessions or rehearsals.

Experimenting with various picking patterns allows you to discover new textures, rhythms, and tones within your guitar composition. Don't hesitate to blend different techniques and styles, as this can lead to a personalized and dynamic approach to your music. Enjoy the process of finding the perfect picking patterns that enhance the rhythmic timing and overall feel of each section in your composition.

LAYER RHYTHMIC ELEMENTS

Layer multiple rhythmic elements within a section. For example, combine a steady bass line with syncopated chords or integrate melodic lines with intricate rhythmic patterns.

EFFECTIVE RHYTHMIC LAYERING

Layering multiple rhythmic elements within a section of your guitar composition is a powerful technique that adds depth, complexity, and a rich sense of texture to your music. By carefully combining various rhythmic elements, you can create a dynamic and engaging listening experience.

Understand the Core Rhythm:

Listening Tip: Establish a primary rhythmic pattern that serves as the foundation for your section.

Identify Complementary Elements:

Listening Tip: Identify additional rhythmic patterns or embellishments that can complement and enhance the core rhythm.

LAYERING TECHNIQUES

Technique 1:

Use Syncopation – Introduce syncopated accents or offbeat hits that contrast with the primary rhythm.

Technique 2:

Cross-Rhythms - Overlay different rhythmic patterns that create interesting intersections and points of tension.

Technique 3:

Polyrhythms - Experiment with simultaneous rhythms with different time signatures to create a layered, intricate feel.

Technique 4:

Counterpoint - Introduce a contrasting melodic or rhythmic line that interacts with the main rhythm.

Technique 5:

Percussive Elements - Incorporate percussive techniques, such as tapping, slapping, or palm muting, to add rhythmic complexity.

EXAMPLE OF LAYERING

Start with a basic strumming pattern (core rhythm) and layer it with a fingerstyle arpeggio pattern (complementary element). The contrast between the two creates a textured sound.

Selective Layering:

Listening Tip: Be selective about when to introduce additional rhythmic elements. Choose moments where the layering enhances the emotional impact of the composition.

Emphasize Transitions:

Listening Tip: Place emphasis on rhythmic changes during transitions between sections. This keeps the listener engaged and provides a clear sense of movement.

Dynamic Layering:

Technique: Gradually introduce or remove layers to create a sense of dynamics within the section.

Listening Tip: Experiment with starting with a sparse arrangement and gradually adding layers as the section progresses.

Explore Different Textures:

Listening Tip: Layering allows you to create different textures within a section. Experiment with blending clean, sustained chords with muted, staccato patterns.

Melodic and Rhythmic Integration:

Technique: Integrate melodic elements that echo or complement the rhythm.

Listening Tip: Use a melodic line that aligns with certain accent points in the rhythmic pattern.

Combining Picking Styles:

Technique: Combine various picking styles (fingerstyle, flatpicking, etc.) to create a diverse rhythmic palette.

Listening Tip: Alternate between fingerstyle picking and strumming to add layers to a chord progression.

Rhythmic Call and Response:

Technique: Establish a rhythmic pattern and respond to it with a contrasting or complementary rhythm.

Listening Tip: Create a dialogue between different rhythmic elements, enhancing the overall musical conversation.

Drone Notes or Chords:

Technique: Include a sustained drone note or chord that provides a constant backdrop to the changing rhythms.

Listening Tip: The drone element adds stability and cohesion to the section.

Use of Pedals and Effects:

Technique: Experiment with sustain pedals, delays, and reverbs to create layered and atmospheric rhythmic effects.

Listening Tip: Tailor the length and intensity of the effects to suit the overall mood of the composition.

Rhythmic Breaks and Pauses:

Technique: Include intentional breaks or pauses in the rhythmic layers to create moments of tension and release.

Listening Tip: These breaks can be effective before transitioning into a new rhythmic pattern.

Recording and Adjusting:

Listening Tip: Record and listen back to ensure that each layer is audible and contributes positively to the overall sound. Adjust the mix to balance the layers effectively.

Collaborate for Layering Ideas:

Listening Tip: If collaborating with other musicians, encourage them to contribute ideas for layering rhythmic elements. Their input can bring fresh perspectives and enhance the complexity of the composition.

Layering multiple rhythmic elements within a section requires careful consideration of how each component interacts with the others. The key is to strike a balance between complexity and coherence, ensuring that the layers work together harmoniously to serve the overarching musical narrative. Enjoy the creative process of experimenting with different rhythmic layers, and let your intuition guide you in crafting a section that captivates your audience.

CONTRAST BETWEEN SECTIONS

Establish contrasting rhythmic patterns between different sections of your composition. This contrast helps define each section and contributes to the overall structure.

CREATING CONTRAST BETWEEN SECTIONS

Establishing contrasting rhythmic patterns between different sections of your guitar composition is a powerful way to create dynamic shifts and maintain listener engagement. This technique helps differentiate various parts of your composition, providing a sense of progression and variation.

Read on to learn how to create contrasting rhythmic sections in your guitar composition.

Define the Core Rhythm for Each Section:

Listening Tip: Clearly define the primary rhythmic pattern for each section. This core rhythm serves as the foundation.

Identify the Emotional Tone of Each Section:

Listening Tip: Consider the emotional tone or mood you want to convey in each section. Rhythmic choices can influence the overall feel.

CONTRAST TEMPO AND TIME SIGNATURES

Technique 1:

Vary the tempo between sections to create a sense of acceleration or deceleration.

Technique 2:

Experiment with different time signatures to alter the rhythmic feel significantly.

Example of Contrasting Rhythmic Patterns:

Example: If the verse has a laid-back, swung feel with a slow tempo, contrast it with a chorus that has a faster-paced, driving rhythm. This dynamic shift adds impact.

Distinguish Chord Progressions:

Technique: Use distinct chord progressions for each section, and tailor the rhythmic pattern to enhance the unique qualities of the chords.

Vary Strumming Patterns and Picking Styles:

Technique: Change strumming patterns or picking styles between sections to create a noticeable shift.

Listening Tip: Experiment with fingerstyle picking in one section and switch to a percussive strumming pattern in another.

Rhythmic Density and Complexity:

Technique: Adjust the rhythmic density and complexity to suit the energy level you want for each section.

Listening Tip: Increase rhythmic complexity in intense or climactic sections, and simplify for more relaxed parts.

Syncopation and Accentuation:

Technique: Introduce syncopated rhythms or emphasize different beats between sections.

Listening Tip: Accentuating the offbeat in one section can contrast with a section that focuses on strong downbeats.

Explore Different Subdivisions:

Technique: Experiment with varied subdivisions of the beat (e.g., eighth notes, triplets, sixteenth notes) to create rhythmic diversity.

Listening Tip: Switching between subdivisions adds interest and keeps the listener engaged.

Dynamic Changes in Articulation:

Technique: Alter the articulation of notes by varying dynamics, staccato vs. legato, or using different articulation techniques.

Listening Tip: A sudden shift from legato to staccato can signal a change in mood or intensity.

Rhythmic Breaks and Pauses:

Technique: Introduce breaks or pauses in the rhythmic flow between sections for added contrast and anticipation.

Listening Tip: A well-timed pause can build tension before a new rhythmic pattern emerges.

Layer Percussive Elements:

Technique: Incorporate percussive elements like muted strums, slaps, or taps to create rhythmic contrast.

Listening Tip: Percussive elements can be particularly effective in transition sections or leading into a chorus.

Contrasting Percussion and Drum Patterns:

Technique: Coordinate guitar rhythms with distinct drum patterns in each section.

Listening Tip: A change in drumming style can signal a shift in rhythmic character.

Rhythmic Call and Response:

Technique: Establish a rhythmic pattern in one section and respond to it with a contrasting or complementary rhythm in the next.

Listening Tip: This technique creates a dialogue between different rhythmic elements.

Recording and Adjusting:

Listening Tip: Record and listen to the transitions between sections. Adjust the rhythmic elements to ensure a smooth and effective contrast.

Collaborate for Rhythmic Ideas:

Listening Tip: If collaborating with other musicians, discuss and experiment with rhythmic ideas together. Collaborators may bring fresh perspectives to the contrast between sections.

Establishing contrasting rhythmic patterns between sections adds a dynamic dimension to your guitar composition, making it more engaging and memorable. Pay attention to the flow and emotional narrative of your music, and let the rhythmic choices enhance the overall impact of each section.

Enjoy the creative process of crafting distinctive rhythmic landscapes that captivate your audience throughout the journey of your composition.

RHYTHMS AND MELODIC PHRASING

Align your rhythmic patterns with the phrasing of the melody or main thematic material. This coordination enhances the musical cohesion between melody and rhythm.

MATCHING RHYTHMS TO MELODIC PHRASING

Aligning your rhythmic patterns with the phrasing of the melody or main thematic material in each section of a guitar composition is crucial for creating a cohesive and well-integrated musical experience. This synchronization enhances the overall impact and musicality of your composition.

Understand Melodic Phrasing:

Listening Tip: Carefully analyze the natural phrasing and accents within your melody or thematic material. Identify key points of emphasis.

Identify Key Phrasing Elements:

Technique: Highlight significant melodic elements, such as the beginning of phrases, important intervals, or climactic moments.

Listening Tip: The peaks and valleys of the melody often align with rhythmic emphasis.

Rhythmic Emphasis on Melodic Peaks:

Technique: Place rhythmic accents or strong beats at the peaks of melodic phrases to enhance their impact.

Example: If the melody rises to a high note, emphasize that note with a strong downbeat or percussive strumming pattern.

Syncopation and Melodic Flow:

Technique: Use syncopated rhythms that complement the natural flow of the melody.

Example: Syncopate strumming or picking patterns to create a sense of forward motion during melodic ascent or descent.

Rhythmic Mimicry of Melodic Patterns:

Technique: Mimic the rhythmic patterns of the melody with your guitar playing.

Example: If the melody has a rhythmic motif like short-short-long, mirror that motif in your accompanying chords or arpeggios.

Phrase-Ending Rhythmic Resolution:

Technique: Align rhythmic resolutions with the ends of melodic phrases for a satisfying conclusion.

Example: If the melody concludes with a long, sustained note, end your accompanying chords with a similar sense of resolution.

Dynamic Contrasts in Sync with Melody:

Technique: Coordinate dynamic changes in your rhythmic patterns with the dynamic shifts in the melody.

Example: If the melody swells in intensity, match that with a dynamic increase in your strumming or picking.

Call and Response Between Melody and Rhythm:

Technique: Establish a call-and-response relationship between the melody and rhythmic patterns.

Example: If the melody introduces a melodic idea, respond with a rhythmic variation that complements or contrasts.

Anticipate Melodic Accents:

Technique: Anticipate accent points in the melody with rhythmic anticipations or leading patterns.

Example: If the melody has a strong accent on a specific beat, prepare the listener by emphasizing that beat with a preceding upbeat strum or pick.

Emphasize Chord Changes with Melody:

Technique: Align chord changes with significant moments in the melody.

Example: Change chords at points where the melody transitions to a new note or when a harmonic shift occurs.

Explore Rhythmic Variations:

Technique: Experiment with variations of rhythmic patterns while staying in sync with the melodic phrasing.

Example: Play with different strumming patterns or picking techniques, adapting them to the changing contours of the melody.

Use of Punctuation for Melodic Highlights:

Technique: Use rhythmic punctuation (pauses or staccato notes) to highlight specific melodic elements.

Example: Introduce a brief pause or staccato strumming on a pivotal note in the melody for added emphasis.

Recording and Adjusting:

Listening Tip: Record your composition and listen for the alignment of rhythmic patterns with the melody. Adjust as needed to achieve optimal synchronization.

Collaborate for Integration:

Listening Tip: If collaborating with other musicians, ensure that everyone is aware of the melodic phrasing. Collaborators can then contribute rhythmically in a way that complements the melody.

Aligning rhythmic patterns with the phrasing of the melody creates a musical synergy that enhances the expressiveness and coherence of your guitar composition. Strive for a seamless integration where rhythm and melody work together to convey the intended emotions and narrative. Enjoy the process of crafting a musical dialogue between your rhythmic accompaniment and the central melodic elements.

RESTS AND DYNAMICS

Incorporate rests strategically to create moments of silence and dynamics. Well-placed rests contribute to the overall rhythmic dynamics of your composition.

UTILIZING RESTS FOR DYNAMICS

Incorporating rests strategically in your guitar composition is a powerful way to create moments of silence, adding dynamics, tension, and a sense of anticipation to your music. By carefully placing rests, you can enhance the overall expressiveness and impact of each section.

Understand the Role of Rests:

Listening Tip: Recognize the significance of rests in music. They are not merely pauses but integral elements that contribute to the overall rhythm and feel.

Identify Natural Breaks in Phrasing:

Technique: Locate points in your melody or thematic material where natural breaks or pauses occur.

Listening Tip: Melodic phrases often have inherent moments where a brief pause feels organic.

Create Contrast with Silence:

Technique: Use rests to create contrast between active, rhythmic sections and moments of silence.

Example: After a lively strumming pattern, introduce a brief rest to allow the sound to settle before moving into the next phrase.

Rests for Emphasis:

Technique: Place rests before or after important melodic or harmonic elements for emphasis.

Example: Follow a powerful chord progression with a brief rest before introducing a delicate, single-note melody.

Silence Before Climactic Moments:

Technique: Introduce a rest just before a climactic moment to build anticipation.

Example: Pause briefly before a soaring guitar solo or a high-intensity strumming pattern.

Use of Syncopated Rests:

Technique: Experiment with syncopated rests to create rhythmic interest.

Example: Instead of resting on a downbeat, place a short rest on an upbeat to add an unexpected rhythmic twist.

Rests as Breath Marks:

Technique: Think of rests as musical breaths, allowing your composition to breathe naturally.

Example: Introduce a rest after a series of intricate phrases to give the listener a moment to absorb the musical content.

Punctuating Transitions with Rests:

Technique: Use rests to punctuate transitions between different sections.

Example: Insert a brief pause when moving from a verse to a chorus, creating a clear distinction between the two parts.

Rests for Dynamic Variation:

Technique: Utilize rests as a tool for dynamic variation within a section.

Example: Start with a section featuring continuous strumming, then introduce rests to gradually decrease intensity.

Rests in Call-and-Response:

Technique: Employ rests in call-and-response patterns to enhance the conversational quality.

Example: After a melodic phrase, allow a moment of rest before the responsive rhythmic accompaniment.

Rests in Percussive Techniques:

Technique: If incorporating percussive techniques, use rests to accentuate beats.

Example: Apply palm muting with intermittent rests to create a percussive, staccato effect.

Creating Suspense with Extended Rests:

Technique: Experiment with longer rests to build suspense.

Example: Follow a section with a dramatic pause before unveiling a new thematic element.

Recording and Adjusting:

Listening Tip: Record your composition and pay attention to the impact of rests. Adjust the timing and duration of rests to achieve the desired effect.

Collaborate for Rest Integration:

Listening Tip: If collaborating with other musicians, ensure that everyone is aware of the planned rests. Collaborators can contribute to creating a unified sense of silence.

Explore Varied Rest Lengths:

Technique: Experiment with different rest lengths for diverse effects.

Example: A short rest might create a sense of tension, while a longer rest can provide a moment of reflection.

Incorporating rests strategically into your guitar composition requires a keen awareness of the rhythmic flow and a thoughtful consideration of the emotional impact you want to convey. Embrace the silence as a musical tool, allowing it to enhance the dynamics and storytelling within your composition. Enjoy the creative process of finding the perfect balance between sound and silence in your musical narrative.

POLYRHYTHMS

Explore polyrhythmic elements by layering conflicting rhythmic patterns. Polyrhythms can add complexity and interest, particularly in more experimental or progressive styles.

EXPERIMENTING WITH POLYRHYTHMS

Exploring polyrhythmic elements in your guitar composition adds a layer of complexity and intrigue to the rhythmic texture. Polyrhythms involve the simultaneous use of different, conflicting rhythmic patterns, creating a sense of rhythmic tension and diversity.

Read on to learn about exploring polyrhythmic elements by layering conflicting rhythmic patterns.

Understand Polyrhythms:

Listening Tip: Familiarize yourself with the concept of polyrhythms by listening to compositions that feature conflicting rhythmic patterns.

Identify the Base Rhythm:

Technique: Establish a base rhythm or time signature that serves as the foundation.

Example: Begin with a straightforward 4/4 time signature.

Layer a Conflicting Rhythm:

Technique: Introduce a second rhythm with a different time signature or subdivision that conflicts with the base rhythm.

Example: Overlay a 3/4 time signature on top of the existing 4/4 rhythm.

Coordinate Downbeats and Accents:

Technique: Coordinate downbeats and accents between the conflicting rhythms to create points of synchronization.

Example: Align the accented beats of both rhythms periodically to maintain a sense of cohesion.

Explore Subdivisions:

Technique: Experiment with conflicting subdivisions, such as triplets against straight eighth notes.

Example: Play triplets on one layer while maintaining a regular eighth-note pattern on another.

Use Syncopation in One Layer:

Technique: Apply syncopation in one layer while keeping the other layer rhythmically straightforward.

Example: Syncopate the accents in a 5/4 layer while maintaining a steady 4/4 pulse in another.

Polymeter vs. Polyrhythm:

Concept: Differentiate between polymeter (different time signatures) and polyrhythm (conflicting rhythms within the same time signature). Experiment with both.

Example: Play in 5/4 against 4/4 (polyrhythm) or alternate between bars of 5/4 and 4/4 (polymeter).

Contrasting Dynamics in Layers:

Technique: Vary the dynamics between the conflicting rhythmic layers for added interest.

Example: Play one layer softly while emphasizing the accents in the other layer.

Experiment with Rhythmic Ratios:

Technique: Create rhythmic ratios by dividing one layer into a different number of subdivisions than the other.

Example: Play quarter notes in one layer against triplets in another.

Shift Phasing:

Technique: Gradually shift the phase of one layer against the other, creating evolving polyrhythmic patterns.

Example: Start with synchronized layers and gradually introduce a delay in one of the patterns.

Apply Articulation Techniques:

Technique: Experiment with different articulation techniques, such as legato, staccato, or percussive hits, in each layer.

Example: Play a legato phrase in one layer while using staccato accents in the other.

Combine Plucking and Strumming:

Technique: Combine fingerstyle plucking with strumming to introduce polyrhythmic elements.

Example: Pluck individual notes in a triplet pattern while simultaneously strumming chords in a 4/4 pattern.

Recording and Adjusting:

Listening Tip: Record your polyrhythmic exploration and listen for the interaction between conflicting patterns. Adjust timing and dynamics for optimal balance.

Collaborate for Polyrhythmic Ideas:

Listening Tip: If collaborating with other musicians, discuss and experiment with polyrhythmic ideas together. Collaborators may bring unique perspectives to the layering process.

Create Melodic Phrases Within Polyrhythms:

Technique: Develop melodic phrases that align with or contrast against the polyrhythmic layers.

Example: Play a melodic line in 7/8 that aligns with the accents of a conflicting 4/4 rhythm.

Gradual Intensity Changes:

Technique: Gradually increase or decrease the intensity of one layer to create dynamic shifts within the polyrhythmic structure.

Example: Introduce a second layer gradually, building intensity throughout a section.

EXAMPLES OF POLYRHYTHMS IN GUITAR COMPOSITION

Tool – Schism:

Polyrhythm:

The main riff features a polyrhythm with a 5:4 ratio, creating a distinctive and complex rhythmic feel.

Meshuggah – Bleed:

Polyrhythm:

Meshuggah often employs complex polyrhythms, such as the 4:3 polyrhythm in the main riff of *Bleed*.

Steve Reich – Electric Counterpoint:

Polyrhythm:

In minimalist composer Steve Reich's work, *Electric Counterpoint*, polyrhythmic elements are used to create intricate layers of sound.

APPLICATION ACROSS GENRES

Progressive Metal:

Example:

Polyphia incorporates polyrhythms into their progressive metal compositions, showcasing technical prowess and rhythmic complexity.

Jazz Fusion:

Example:

Allan Holdsworth's jazz fusion compositions often feature polyrhythmic elements, adding a layer of sophistication to the music.

Example:

World music genres, such as West African drumming, commonly utilize polyrhythms to create intricate and vibrant rhythmic patterns.

76

Exploring polyrhythmic elements can lead to captivating and intricate rhythmic landscapes in your guitar composition. Embrace the challenge of combining conflicting patterns and enjoy the unique energy and depth that polyrhythms bring to your music. Remember to balance complexity with clarity, ensuring that the layers work together to enhance the overall musical experience.

DOTTED RHYTHMS

Introduce dotted rhythms to add emphasis to specific notes or beats. Dotted rhythms create a sense of elongation and can be used to highlight important moments.

USING DOTTED RHYTHMS FOR EMPHASIS

Dotted rhythms involve the use of a dot placed after a note to extend its duration by half. This creates a rhythmic pattern where the first note is followed by a shorter, staccato note. For example, a dotted quarter note followed by an eighth note in 4/4 time would be equivalent to three eighth notes.

INTRODUCING DOTTED RHYTHMS

Understanding Dotted Rhythms:
Definition: A dotted rhythm consists of a note (e.g., quarter or half note) followed by a dot, extending its duration by half. The dot is then followed by a shorter note (e.g., eighth or sixteenth note).

Adding Emphasis with Dotted Rhythms:
Technique: Use dotted rhythms to emphasize specific beats or notes within a phrase.

Example: In a 4/4 time signature, replace a simple quarter note with a dotted quarter note followed by an eighth note to emphasize the first beat.

Creating Syncopation:

Technique: Introduce dotted rhythms on offbeats to create syncopation and rhythmic interest.

Example: Place a dotted eighth note on the "and" of a beat, followed by a sixteenth note, creating a syncopated feel.

Adding Swing Feel:

Technique: Apply dotted rhythms to create a swing feel by emphasizing the first note in each pair.

Example: Replace even eighth notes with dotted eighth-sixteenth note pairs to infuse swing into a section.

Varying Note Lengths:

Technique: Experiment with different note lengths in dotted rhythm patterns for dynamic contrast.

Example: Alternate between dotted quarter notes and dotted half notes to create a varied rhythmic texture.

Enhancing Melodic Phrasing:

Technique: Use dotted rhythms to highlight specific notes in a melodic line.

Example: Apply a dotted rhythm to a crucial melodic note, creating a moment of emphasis within the phrase.

Combining Dotted Rhythms with Chords:

Technique: Apply dotted rhythms to chordal accompaniment to add rhythmic flair.

Example: Play a chord with a dotted rhythm, such as a dotted half note followed by a quarter note, for a percussive effect.

Dotted Rhythms in Fingerstyle Techniques:

Technique: Experiment with dotted rhythms in fingerstyle playing, varying the attack on each note.

Example: Use a dotted rhythm pattern in fingerstyle to create a nuanced and expressive performance.

Building Rhythmic Tension:

Technique: Use dotted rhythms strategically to build tension before resolving to a more straightforward rhythm.

Example: Employ a series of dotted rhythms leading into a section with a regular rhythmic pattern for a climactic effect.

Combining Dotted Rhythms with Rests:

Technique: Integrate rests alongside dotted rhythms to create dynamic pauses.

Example: Use a dotted rhythm followed by a rest to create a short, impactful silence within a rhythmic sequence.

Recording and Adjusting:

Listening Tip: Record your composition to evaluate the impact of dotted rhythms. Adjust the timing and duration to achieve the desired emphasis and feel.

Collaborating with Other Instruments:

Listening Tip: If collaborating with other musicians, ensure that the placement of dotted rhythms aligns with the overall rhythmic context. Collaborators can enhance the collective impact of the dotted patterns.

Incorporating dotted rhythms into your guitar composition adds a layer of sophistication, allowing you to emphasize specific beats, create rhythmic interest, and contribute to the overall expressiveness of your music. Enjoy the creative possibilities that dotted rhythms bring to your compositions.

ADAPTING RHYTHMS

Consider the techniques you plan to use on the guitar, such as hammer-ons, pull-offs, slides, and tapping. Adapt your rhythmic patterns to incorporate these techniques for added expressiveness.

ADAPT RHYTHMS TO GUITAR TECHNIQUES

Adapting rhythms to guitar techniques is an essential aspect of crafting engaging and playable compositions. The guitar offers a wide range of techniques, from strumming and picking to fingerstyle and percussive elements.

Understand Guitar Techniques:

Definition: Familiarize yourself with common guitar techniques such as strumming, picking, fingerstyle, hammer-ons, pull-offs, slides, bends, and percussive elements.

Example: Recognize the difference between a picked note and a hammered-on note.

Identify the Primary Guitar Technique:

Technique Integration: Determine the primary technique for a section based on the desired sound and feel.

Example: If aiming for a percussive sound, focus on incorporating tapping and slapping techniques.

Align Rhythms with Strumming Patterns:

Strumming Integration: Adapt rhythms to complement strumming patterns, ensuring a smooth and coordinated motion.

Example: Use downstrokes for emphasized beats and upstrokes for lighter, offbeat accents in a strumming pattern.

Coordinate Picking Patterns:

Picking Integration: Align rhythmic patterns with picking techniques, emphasizing specific notes for clarity.

Example: Apply alternate picking for even-note subdivisions and directional picking for melodic phrases.

Sync Rhythms with Fingerstyle Techniques:

Fingerstyle Integration: Integrate rhythmic patterns with fingerstyle techniques, assigning distinct roles to each finger.

Example: Use the thumb for bass notes and fingers for melody, coordinating with the rhythmic structure.

Explore Percussive Elements:

Percussive Integration: Incorporate rhythmic elements through percussive techniques like tapping, slapping, or muted strums.

Example: Introduce percussive slaps on the guitar body between chords to enhance the rhythmic groove.

Match Rhythms with Slide and Bend Movements:

Slide/Bend Integration: Coordinate rhythmic patterns with slide or bend movements for expressive phrasing.

Example: Apply a slide on a sustained note to add a rhythmic and tonal dynamic.

Adapt to Hammer-Ons and Pull-Offs:

Hammer-On/Pull-Off Integration: Adjust rhythms to accommodate hammer-ons and pull-offs seamlessly.

Example: Integrate hammer-ons for quick, legato passages and pull-offs for descending melodic lines.

Combine Techniques for Versatility:

Technique Combination: Experiment with combining different techniques within a rhythmic context for added versatility.

Example: Blend fingerstyle picking with percussive taps on the guitar body for a diverse rhythmic texture.

Vary Strumming Dynamics:

Dynamic Strumming: Vary the dynamics within strumming patterns to create a nuanced and expressive rhythm.

Example: Use controlled strums for softer sections and vigorous strums for more intense moments.

Incorporate Staccato and Legato Playing:

Articulation Integration: Adjust rhythmic patterns to include staccato and legato elements for articulative diversity.

Example: Apply staccato strums for short, punchy accents and legato phrasing for smooth, connected passages.

Recording and Adjusting:

Listening Tip: Record your composition and pay attention to the interaction between rhythmic patterns and guitar techniques. Adjust the timing and intensity to achieve a balanced and coherent performance.

Collaborate for Technique Enhancement:

Collaborative Approach: If collaborating with other musicians, discuss and experiment with various techniques to enhance the collective impact of the composition.

Adapting rhythms to guitar techniques involves a thoughtful integration of rhythmic patterns with the diverse capabilities of the guitar. Embrace the versatility of the instrument and explore creative combinations of techniques to elevate the rhythmic dynamics of your composition. As you experiment, pay attention to the playability of the guitar parts to ensure an enjoyable and fluid performance.

PERCUSSIVE QUALITIES OF THE GUITAR

Leverage the percussive qualities of the guitar. Incorporate muted strums, slaps, or percussive taps to enhance the rhythmic texture.

CONSIDERING THE GUITAR'S PERCUSSIVE QUALITIES

Leveraging the percussive qualities of the guitar is a fantastic way to add rhythmic flair and dynamic interest to your composition. The percussive elements can emulate the sounds of drums and enhance the overall groove of your music.

Understand Percussive Techniques:

Technique Exploration: Familiarize yourself with percussive techniques on the guitar, including tapping, slapping, body percussion, and muted strums.

Example: Experiment with tapping on the guitar body to create a rhythmic pulse.

Identify Percussive Opportunities:

Section Analysis: Identify sections in your composition where percussive elements can complement or replace traditional strumming or picking.

Example: Consider using percussive hits during instrumental breaks or transitions.

Incorporate Body Percussion:

Body Integration: Utilize the guitar body for percussion by tapping, slapping, or knocking to create rhythmic accents.

Example: Incorporate a percussive slap on the guitar body between chord changes for added rhythmic emphasis.

Enhance Strumming Patterns:

Strumming Enhancement: Integrate muted strums and slaps into strumming patterns to elevate the percussive qualities.

Example: Combine regular strums with muted strums to create a rhythmic, percussive groove.

Tap for Rhythmic Pulse:

Tapping Dynamics: Add tapping to your playing technique, using it as a rhythmic pulse or to accent specific beats.

Example: Tap on the guitar's top with your fingertips while maintaining a steady strumming pattern.

Explore Slap Techniques:

Slap Integration: Experiment with slapping the strings to create percussive sounds, adding a rhythmic and dynamic element.

Example: Use slaps on the lower strings to mark the downbeats in a rhythmic sequence.

Combine Percussive Hits with Chords:

Chord Integration: Combine chord progressions with percussive hits to create a rhythmic and harmonic blend.

Example: Play a chord followed by a percussive hit, enhancing the rhythm between chord changes.

Create Percussive Breaks:

Break Dynamics: Design sections where the guitar takes on a percussive role, creating breaks or interludes.

Example: Use muted strums and body percussion for a short, percussive break between verses.

Experiment with Muted Strums:

Muted Strumming: Integrate muted strums to create a percussive, staccato effect.

Example: Play a rhythmic pattern using muted strums to punctuate the dynamics of a section.

Coordinate Percussion with Melody:

Melody Integration: Coordinate percussive hits with melodic phrases, enhancing both rhythm and melody.

Example: Combine tapping on the guitar body with a melodic line played on the higher strings.

Vary Percussive Intensity:

Dynamic Variation: Vary the intensity of percussive hits to match the dynamics of different sections.

Example: Increase percussive intensity during a build-up or climax in the composition.

Recording and Adjusting:

Listening Tip: Record your composition to assess the impact of percussive elements. Adjust the timing and intensity to achieve the desired rhythmic balance.

Collaborate for Percussive Creativity:

Collaborative Approach: If collaborating with other musicians, explore creative percussive ideas together to enhance the overall rhythm and groove.

Leveraging the percussive qualities of the guitar adds a unique dimension to your composition, transforming it into a rhythmic powerhouse. Experiment with various percussive techniques and find ways to seamlessly integrate them into different sections of your composition, ensuring a dynamic and engaging musical experience.

TIME SIGNATURE CHANGES

Experiment with changes in time signatures between sections or within a section. Time signature changes can add a sense of unpredictability and keep the listener engaged.

EXPERIMENTING WITH TIME SIGNATURE CHANGES

Experimenting with changes in time signatures can bring a rich and dynamic quality to your guitar composition. Shifting between time signatures adds a sense of unpredictability and can contribute to the overall mood and structure of your piece.

Let's explore how to experiment with changes in time signatures within and between sections.

UNDERSTANDING TIME SIGNATURES

Time Signature Basics:

Familiarize yourself with different time signatures, including common ones like 4/4, 3/4, 6/8, and more.

Example: Recognize that a time signature like 4/4 indicates four beats per measure, while 3/4 signifies three beats.

Map Out Your Composition:

Structural Planning: Outline the structure of your composition and identify points where a change in time signature could enhance the musical narrative.

Example: Consider transitioning to a 6/8 time signature during a bridge section for a contrasting feel.

Experimenting Within Sections:

Intra-section Changes: Introduce changes in time signatures within a single section to create dynamic shifts.

Example: Start a verse in 4/4 and seamlessly transition to 7/8 for a few measures before returning to 4/4.

Enhance Rhythmic Feel:

Emotional Impact: Experiment with time signature changes to evoke specific emotions or enhance the rhythmic feel.

Example: Switching from 4/4 to 5/4 can add tension and excitement, especially if aligned with a climactic moment.

Create Smooth Transitions:

Transition Techniques: Develop smooth transitions between different time signatures to maintain a cohesive flow.

Example: Use a brief drum fill or a sustained chord to ease the listener into the new time signature.

Align Changes with Lyrics or Melody:

Lyric/Melody Connection: Align time signature changes with specific lyrical or melodic phrases to enhance musical expression.

Example: Shift to 3/4 during a reflective lyric or a slower melodic passage.

Use Odd Time Signatures for Intrigue:

Odd Meters: Experiment with odd time signatures (e.g., 5/4, 7/8) for a sense of intrigue and unpredictability.

Example: Incorporate a section in 7/8 to create an unconventional rhythmic feel.

Maintain Groove and Pulse:

Groove Preservation: Ensure that changes in time signatures do not compromise the overall groove and pulse of the composition.

Example: Transition smoothly from a funk-inspired 7/8 section back to a more conventional 4/4 groove.

Consider Tempo Changes:

Tempo Dynamics: Explore changes in tempo alongside shifts in time signatures to enhance the impact.

Example: Gradually increase the tempo as you shift from 4/4 to 5/4 for added intensity.

Experimenting Between Sections:

Inter-section Changes: Introduce new time signatures when transitioning between different sections of your composition.

Example: Move from a verse in 6/8 to a chorus in 4/4 for a contrasting and dynamic effect.

Dynamic Drum Patterns:

Drum Integration: Work closely with your drummer or use drum programming to create dynamic patterns that highlight the changes in time signatures.

Example: Utilize intricate drum fills during transitions to signal upcoming changes.

Recording and Adjusting:

Listening Tip: Record your composition and listen for the impact of time signature changes. Adjust timing and transitions as needed for optimal cohesion.

Collaborate for Musical Synergy:

Collaborative Approach: If working with other musicians, discuss and experiment collaboratively to ensure that everyone is comfortable with and enhances the transitions between time signatures.

Experimenting with changes in time signatures is a powerful tool in guitar composition. It allows you to create nuanced and diverse musical landscapes, keeping your audience engaged and intrigued throughout the journey of your composition. Be bold in your exploration, and let the changes in time signatures contribute to the unique identity of your music.

RHYTHMIC CLIMAXES

Build rhythmic climaxes within sections by gradually increasing the intensity and complexity of the rhythmic patterns. This creates a sense of tension and release.

BUILDING RHYTHMIC CLIMAXES

Building rhythmic climaxes in a guitar composition involves creating moments of heightened intensity and excitement, often leading to a musical peak. These climaxes can serve as focal points, capturing the listener's attention and adding emotional impact to your composition.

Plan Climactic Moments:

Structural Awareness: Identify key sections in your composition where a rhythmic climax would be most impactful.

Example: Choose a chorus, bridge, or instrumental break as a potential climax point.

Dynamic Rhythmic Patterns:

Introduce Variations: Develop dynamic rhythmic patterns that escalate in complexity and intensity.

Example: Start with a straightforward rhythm and gradually introduce syncopations, accents, and faster subdivisions.

Utilize Drum Dynamics:

Collaborate with Drummer: Work closely with a drummer or use percussion elements to accentuate and enhance rhythmic climaxes.

Example: Incorporate drum fills, crashes, and increased percussion intensity during climactic moments.

Gradual Tempo Build-Up:

Tempo Dynamics: Gradually increase the tempo leading up to the climax to create a sense of urgency and excitement.

Example: Start a section at a moderate tempo and subtly speed up as you approach the climax.

Layered Rhythmic Elements:

Multi-Instrumental Build-Up: Layer multiple rhythmic elements, such as percussion, bass, and synths, to create a dense and textured sound.

Example: Introduce additional instruments playing rhythmic counterpoints as you build towards the climax.

Syncopation and Offbeat Accents:

Offbeat Emphasis: Experiment with syncopated rhythms and offbeat accents to add a sense of unpredictability.

Example: Introduce a section where guitar chords or phrases land on offbeats, creating tension.

Crescendo in Dynamics:

Dynamic Swells: Use a gradual crescendo in dynamics, starting softly and increasing the volume as you approach the climax.

Example: Play the initial measures of a section softly and then progressively play with increasing intensity.

Rhythmic Punctuation:

Percussive Hits: Employ percussive hits or staccato chords strategically to punctuate the rhythm and signal the climax.

Example: Use muted strums or palm-muted chords leading into the climactic moment.

Building Complexity in Phrasing:

Phrasing Evolution: Increase the complexity of your guitar phrasing as you approach the climax, incorporating more intricate rhythmic patterns.

Example: Gradually introduce arpeggios, fast scale runs, or rhythmic variations in lead guitar lines.

Layered Harmonies:

Harmonic Depth: Introduce layered harmonies during the climax to add depth and richness to the rhythmic intensity.

Example: Play harmonized guitar lines or add backing vocals for a fuller sound.

Contrast with Previous Sections:

Sectional Contrast: Ensure that the climactic section contrasts with preceding parts, making the peak more noticeable.

Example: If the verses are relatively simple, make the rhythmic climax more intricate and intense.

Unleash Energy with Chord Progressions:

Powerful Chords: Utilize powerful and emotive chord progressions during the climax to evoke strong emotional responses.

Example: Build tension with suspended chords or dissonant progressions leading into a resolution.

Articulate with Articulation Techniques:

Expressive Articulation: Use varied articulation techniques such as slides, bends, and vibrato to add expressiveness to climactic phrases.

Example: Apply a wide, expressive vibrato to sustained notes during the climax.

Recording and Adjusting:

Listening Tip: Record your composition and pay close attention to the effectiveness of the rhythmic climaxes. Adjust elements as needed for maximum impact.

Collaborate for Maximum Impact:

Collaborative Approach: If working with other musicians, communicate and collaborate to ensure a collective build-up to the rhythmic climax, creating a unified impact.

Building rhythmic climaxes requires a strategic combination of tempo changes, dynamic shifts, and intricate rhythmic patterns. Experiment with these elements, considering the emotional context of your composition, to create powerful and memorable climactic moments in your guitar composition.

THE ART OF ACTIVE LISTENING

Record your playing and listen actively to evaluate the effectiveness of your rhythmic patterns. Adjustments can be made to achieve the desired rhythmic impact.

HOW TO LISTEN ACTIVELY

Listening actively to your guitar composition recordings is a crucial step in refining and enhancing your musical creations. Active listening involves focused and intentional attention to various elements within the recording.

Clear Your Mind:

Mindful Preparation: Before hitting play, clear your mind of distractions to fully engage with the music.

Example: Find a quiet space and eliminate external disturbances.

Set the Right Environment:

Optimal Listening Conditions: Choose an environment with good acoustics and use quality headphones or speakers.

Example: Listen in a room with minimal background noise.

Initial Impression:

First Listen: Allow yourself to experience the composition without overanalyzing on the first listen.

Example: Absorb the overall mood, energy, and emotional impact.

Focus on Specific Elements:

Selective Attention: In subsequent listens, focus on specific elements like guitar technique, dynamics, and tonal qualities.

Example: Listen specifically to the intricacies of your guitar playing technique.

Evaluate Timing and Tempo:

Rhythmic Precision: Assess the timing and tempo to ensure a cohesive and tight performance.

Example: Check if the rhythm section aligns seamlessly with the guitar parts.

Tonal Balance:

Frequency Distribution: Pay attention to tonal balance, ensuring that each instrument occupies its appropriate frequency range.

Example: Make sure the guitar doesn't overpower other instruments in the mix.

Dynamic Range:

Dynamic Variation: Evaluate the dynamic range, ensuring that softer and louder parts contribute to a well-balanced musical narrative.

Example: Check for abrupt volume changes or sections lacking dynamic variation.

Instrument Separation:

Clarity of Instruments: Ensure each instrument is distinct and contributes to the overall texture.

Example. Check if multiple guitar parts or other instruments are clear and not muddled.

Articulation and Phrasing:

Expressive Elements: Assess the articulation and phrasing of each note or chord, considering expressiveness and musicality.

Example: Listen for nuances like slides, bends, and vibrato.

Evaluate Transitions:

Smooth Transitions: Focus on transitions between sections, ensuring they are seamless and well-executed.

Example: Check for smooth changes between verses, choruses, and bridges.

Melodic Clarity:

Melody Audibility: Confirm that the melody is clear and easily discernible.

Example: Ensure that lead guitar lines or vocal melodies are not buried in the mix.

Check for Artifacts:

Recording Quality: Listen for any unwanted artifacts, such as clicks, pops, or distortion.

Example: Scrutinize the recording for any technical issues that may affect the overall listening experience.

Assess Emotional Impact:

Emotional Resonance: Gauge the emotional impact of the composition and whether it aligns with your artistic intention.

Example: Consider how the music makes you feel and whether it conveys the intended mood.

Compare to Reference Tracks:

Reference Listening: Compare your composition to professionally produced tracks in a similar genre.

Example: Use reference tracks to identify areas for improvement and to understand industry standards.

Take Notes:

Document Insights: Jot down notes during and after listening sessions to remember specific areas that need improvement or adjustment.

Example: Note sections that stood out positively or aspects that could be refined.

Iterative Refinement:

Revision Process: Use the insights gained from active listening to iteratively refine and enhance your composition.

Example: Make adjustments to the mix, performance, or arrangement based on your observations.

Active listening is an ongoing and iterative process. Regularly revisit your recordings with fresh ears and a critical mindset to continually improve your guitar compositions. This intentional approach will contribute to the growth and refinement of your musical creations over time.

INSPIRATION FROM GENRES

Draw inspiration from various genres and styles. Explore how rhythmic patterns are used in different musical traditions and adapt them to suit the context of your composition.

SEEK INSPIRATION FROM DIFFERENT GENRES

Drawing inspiration from different genres is an excellent way to infuse creativity and diversity into your guitar compositions. By exploring a variety of musical styles, you can incorporate unique elements, techniques, and perspectives into your own work.

Diversify Your Listening Experience:

Wide Musical Range: Listen to a broad spectrum of genres beyond your comfort zone.

Example: If you primarily play rock, explore jazz, electronic, or world music.

Analyze Unique Instrumentation:

Instrumental Palette: Analyze the instrumentation used in genres you're less familiar with.

Example: Consider the intricate use of brass in jazz or electronic synthesizers in ambient music.

Explore Rhythmic Complexity:

Rhythmic Diversity: Investigate rhythmic patterns and complexities in genres like Afrobeat, Latin, or Indian classical music.

Example: Infuse polyrhythmic elements from Afro-Cuban percussion into your guitar compositions.

Study Harmonic Progressions:

Harmonic Innovation: Study harmonic progressions in genres like jazz or blues.

Example: Experiment with extended chords and modal progressions inspired by jazz.

Embrace Cultural Influences:

Cultural Fusion: Explore music from different cultures to incorporate diverse influences.

Example: Blend flamenco guitar techniques into your composition for a touch of Spanish influence.

Experiment with Time Signatures:

Time Signature Exploration: Borrow time signature ideas from progressive rock or folk genres.

Example: Use 5/4 or 7/8 time signatures to add complexity to your guitar compositions.

Learn Genre-Specific Techniques:

Technique Adaptation: Adopt specific techniques associated with different genres.

Example: Incorporate fingerstyle picking techniques from classical guitar into your playing.

Combine Electronic Elements:

Electronic Fusion: Integrate electronic elements inspired by genres like EDM or synth-pop.

Example: Experiment with synthesizers or electronic effects to create unique textures.

Capture Emotional Expressiveness:

Genre-specific Emotions: Analyze how different genres convey emotions and bring that expressiveness into your playing.

Example: Infuse the melancholic feel of blues into a rock ballad.

Explore Unconventional Scales:

Scale Variety: Explore scales beyond the usual major and minor scales.

Example: Experiment with the Phrygian scale common in flamenco or the Pentatonic scale used in blues.

Fusion of Genres:

Genre Fusion: Combine elements from multiple genres to create a unique hybrid.

Example: Fuse reggae-inspired rhythm with metal guitar riffs for an innovative sound.

Incorporate Storytelling Elements:

Genre Narratives: Learn how genres like folk or country tell stories through their compositions.

Example: Integrate storytelling elements into your lyrics or musical phrasing.

Experiment with Genres in Collaboration:

Collaborative Exploration: Collaborate with musicians from different genres for fresh perspectives.

Example: Work with a jazz saxophonist to add a jazz flavor to your guitar composition.

Attend Live Performances:

Live Inspiration: Attend live performances of diverse genres to witness the energy firsthand.

Example: Experience the excitement of a live jazz ensemble or a classical orchestra.

Stay Open-Minded:

Open Exploration: Keep an open mind and embrace the unexpected in your musical exploration.

Example: Don't be afraid to incorporate elements from a genre you initially might not have considered.

Experiment with Genre Mashups:

Mashup Creativity: Combine elements from two or more genres to create a fresh and unique sound.

Example: Merge bluesy slide guitar with electronic beats for an unconventional blend.

Keep a Musical Journal:

Inspiration Log: Maintain a musical journal where you jot down ideas and inspirations from various genres.

Example: Note down specific techniques or motifs you find interesting.

Create Genre Playlists:

Playlist Curation: Curate playlists featuring songs from different genres to inspire your guitar compositions.

Example: Build playlists for specific moods or creative sessions.

Regularly Revisit Genres:

Ongoing Exploration: Periodically revisit genres you've explored to continuously broaden your musical palette.

Example: Rediscover classic blues or delve into contemporary indie rock.

Collaborate with Musicians from Different Genres:

Cross-Genre Collaboration: Collaborate with musicians specializing in genres different from your own.

Example: Partner with a percussionist skilled in world music for a cross-genre project.

Incorporate Global Influences:

World Music Inspirations: Explore world music genres for unique rhythms, scales, and instrumentation.

Example: Integrate sitar-like melodies or tabla rhythms for a global touch.

Experiment with Genres in Songwriting:

Genre-blending Songwriting: Write songs that seamlessly blend elements from different genres.

Example: Combine folk storytelling with rock instrumentation for a genre-blending composition.

By actively seeking inspiration from various genres, you can enrich your guitar compositions with new ideas, techniques, and creative approaches. Remember that each genre offers a unique perspective.

COLLABORATE WITH DRUMMERS OR PERCUSSIONISTS

If possible, collaborate with drummers or percussionists to enhance the rhythmic elements of your composition. Their input can bring a new dimension to the overall rhythm.

QUESTIONS TO ASK

Collaborating with drummers or percussionists can significantly enhance the rhythmic elements of your guitar composition. Effective communication and understanding between musicians are crucial for a successful collaboration.

Understanding the Composition:

1. What's your initial impression of the composition?
2. Have you identified specific rhythmic elements or patterns that stand out to you?
3. How can we collectively enhance the overall rhythmic feel of the piece?

Discussion on Genre and Style:

1. What genre(s) do you think best describes the composition, and how can we accentuate that through rhythm?
2. Are there specific drumming styles or techniques commonly associated with this genre that we can incorporate?
3. How can we infuse elements from different genres to create a unique rhythmic blend?

Exploring Drum Kit and Percussion Options:

1. Do you envision a full drum kit, or should we incorporate specific percussion instruments?
2. Which percussive elements (e.g., snare, kick, hi-hat, congas) do you think would complement the guitar parts best?
3. Are there any unconventional or ethnic percussion instruments you'd like to experiment with?

Rhythmic Dynamics and Intensity:

1. How would you approach the dynamics of the rhythmic sections in terms of intensity and volume?
2. Are there specific sections where we should build intensity, and others where we should pull back for contrast?
3. Can we experiment with rhythmic variations to keep the energy dynamic throughout the composition?

Tempo and Time Signature Considerations:

1. Do you feel the current tempo suits the composition, or should we experiment with variations?
2. Are there opportunities to explore different time signatures for added rhythmic interest?
3. How can we ensure a tight synchronization between the guitar and percussion in terms of timing?

Individual Instrument Showcase:

1. Are there moments where we can feature specific drum or percussion elements individually for added impact?
2. Can we experiment with solo sections or breaks to highlight the rhythmic prowess of the drums or percussion?
3. How can we balance showcasing individual instruments with contributing to the overall composition?

Creative Rhythmic Interpretation:

1. In which sections can we experiment with creative rhythmic interpretations or improvisation?
2. Are there opportunities for call-and-response patterns between the guitar and percussion?
3. How can we bring a fresh perspective to the rhythmic elements of the composition?

Subtle Nuances and Fills:

1. Where do you envision subtle percussive nuances or fills to add texture without overpowering the guitar parts?
2. Can we discuss how to use fills strategically to enhance transitions between sections?
3. Are there specific rhythmic motifs we can introduce as signature elements?

Feedback Loop and Collaboration Process:

1. How would you prefer to receive feedback during the collaboration process?

2. Are there specific aspects of the guitar composition where you'd like more input or direction?

3. How can we ensure open communication to address any adjustments or refinements needed?

Recording and Production Considerations:

1. What recording techniques or production elements can we incorporate to capture the desired rhythmic ambiance?

2. Are there specific percussion mic placements or drumming styles that could enhance the recording?

3. How can we ensure a balanced mix that highlights both the guitar and percussion elements?

Rehearsal and Performance Aspects:

1. How do you approach rehearsing and preparing for performances with a guitarist?

2. Are there specific rehearsal techniques or routines that you find effective in refining the rhythmic collaboration?

3. What elements contribute to a successful live performance, and how can we ensure a tight connection on stage?

Mutual Goals and Expectations:

1. What are your goals and expectations for the rhythmic collaboration in this composition?

2. How can we align our musical visions to create a cohesive and compelling performance?

3. Are there specific outcomes or achievements you aim for in our collaborative effort?

Open communication and a shared understanding of the rhythmic goals will strengthen the collaboration between guitarists and drummers or percussionists. By asking these questions, you'll establish a solid foundation for a creative and synchronized musical partnership.

ITERATE AND REFINE

Be open to iteration and refinement. Rhythmic patterns may evolve as you play and listen, so continue to refine them until they perfectly complement the musical narrative.

ITERATIVE MINDSET

Being open to iteration and refinement is a key mindset that can significantly elevate the quality and depth of your guitar compositions. Embracing a continuous improvement approach allows you to refine your ideas, experiment with new elements, and ultimately create a more polished and nuanced musical piece.

Embrace the Evolution of Ideas:
Open-mindedness: Understand that initial ideas may transform and evolve during the creative process.

Example: Be willing to let go of preconceived notions and allow your composition to take unexpected turns.

Regularly Review and Reflect:
Scheduled Reflection: Set aside time regularly to review your composition with a fresh perspective.

Example: Take breaks during the creation process to come back with renewed insights.

Seek Feedback and Input:
External Perspectives: Share your composition with trusted peers or mentors to gain valuable feedback.

Example: Actively seek constructive criticism and insights from musicians whose opinions you respect.

Experiment with Alternatives:

Creative Exploration: Be open to trying alternative melodies, harmonies, or arrangements.

Example: Experiment with different chord progressions, rhythms, or tempos to discover new possibilities.

Iterative Refinement:

Step-by-Step Improvements: Break down your composition into smaller sections and refine each part iteratively.

Example: Focus on perfecting one section at a time rather than attempting to refine the entire piece in one go.

Record and Listen Actively:

Critical Listening: Record your playing and actively listen to identify areas that can be refined.

Example: Pay attention to nuances, dynamics, and overall cohesion during playback.

Be Patient with the Process:

Understanding Progress Takes Time: Recognize that achieving the desired result may require multiple iterations.

Example: Patience allows you to approach refinement with a calm and focused mindset.

Celebrate Small Victories:

Acknowledging Improvements: Celebrate small achievements and improvements during the refinement process.

Example: Recognize when a particular section or phrase has reached a level of refinement.

Stay Adaptable to Change:

Adaptability: Be prepared to make changes, even if it means revisiting previously composed sections.

Example: If a new idea enhances the composition, be flexible enough to incorporate it.

Use Technology to Your Advantage:

Digital Tools: Leverage recording software and digital tools to experiment with different arrangements.

Example: Try different virtual instruments or effects to enhance your guitar tones.

Involve Collaborators:

Collective Refinement: Collaborate with other musicians to refine the composition collectively.

Example: Engage in a collaborative process where everyone contributes to the refinement.

Compare Versions:

Side-by-Side Analysis: Keep different versions of your composition and compare them to assess improvements.

Example: Save iterations of your work to track the evolution of the composition.

Challenge Your Comfort Zone:

Exploration Beyond Familiarity: Push yourself to explore ideas or techniques outside your comfort zone.

Example: Experiment with genres or playing styles that are less familiar to you.

Document the Refinement Process:

Journaling: Document the changes made during the refinement process to track your creative journey.

Example: Maintain a composition journal noting what worked, what didn't, and ideas for improvement.

Prioritize Impactful Changes:

Focused Refinement: Prioritize refinement efforts on elements that have the most significant impact.

Example: Identify key sections or motifs that contribute significantly to the composition.

Feedback Loop with Performances:

Live Testing: Perform your composition live and use the experience to identify areas that need further refinement.

Example: Gauge audience reactions and adjust accordingly for subsequent performances.

Maintain a Growth Mindset:

Continuous Learning: View each iteration as an opportunity for growth and learning.

Example: Consider refinement as an ongoing process rather than a final destination.

Trust Your Intuition:

Intuitive Refinement: Trust your musical instincts and intuition during the refinement process.

Example: If a change feels right, explore it further, even if it deviates from the original plan.

Iterative Performance Practice:

Refinement through Practice: Refine your composition through repeated performance practice.

Example: Use practice sessions to address technical challenges and improve overall execution.

Stay Inspired by Others:

External Inspiration: Draw inspiration from the refinement processes of other musicians.

Example: Study how accomplished musicians continually refine their work and adapt it to your own process.

Balancing Self-Critique and Appreciation:

Constructive Self-Critique: Critique your work constructively while also appreciating the unique qualities that make it yours.

Example: Acknowledge both areas for improvement and elements that showcase your personal style.

By cultivating a mindset of iteration and refinement, you ensure that your guitar compositions continue to evolve and reach their fullest potential. This approach not only enhances the quality of your current work but also contributes to your growth as a musician over time.

AUDIENCE ENGAGEMENT

Think about how your rhythmic patterns contribute to audience engagement. A well-crafted rhythm can make your composition memorable and enjoyable for listeners.

CONSIDERING AUDIENCE ENGAGEMENT

Understanding how your rhythmic patterns contribute to audience engagement is crucial for creating a compelling and impactful guitar composition. Rhythm is a powerful element that can evoke emotions, drive energy, and captivate listeners.

Define the Mood and Energy:

Mood Alignment: Consider the mood you intend to convey with your composition. How do your rhythmic patterns align with the desired emotional atmosphere?

Energy Levels: Assess how your rhythms contribute to the overall energy of the piece. Do they create excitement, tension, or relaxation?

Variety in Rhythmic Patterns:

Dynamic Range: Evaluate the diversity of rhythmic patterns used throughout the composition. Are there variations in tempo, time signatures, or rhythmic motifs?

Listener Engagement: Consider how the introduction of new rhythmic elements keeps the audience engaged and interested.

Pacing and Groove:

Effective Pacing: Analyze how the pacing of your rhythmic patterns enhances the flow of the composition. Does it create anticipation or moments of release?

Groove Analysis: Pay attention to the groove created by your rhythmic patterns. How does it influence the audience's physical response or inclination to move with the music?

Align with Cultural Influences:

Cultural Connection: If your composition draws from specific cultural influences, assess how your rhythmic patterns align with those cultural elements. Are there rhythms that resonate with a particular cultural context?

Cross-Cultural Appeal: Consider how your rhythms might appeal to a broader audience by incorporating diverse cultural elements.

Interactive Rhythmic Phrasing:

Call-and-Response: Explore how call-and-response rhythmic phrasing engages the audience. Does it create a dialogue between the guitar and the listener?

Participation: Consider whether certain rhythmic patterns invite the audience to mentally or physically participate in the music.

Rhythmic Tension and Release:

Build Tension Strategically: Assess how your rhythmic patterns contribute to the buildup of tension within the composition. How are these tensions released, and how does it impact the listener's experience?

Emotional Resonance: Consider how moments of rhythmic release or resolution align with emotional peaks in the composition.

Syncopation and Offbeat Accents:

Syncopated Rhythms: Explore the use of syncopation and offbeat accents. How do these rhythmic elements add interest and surprise to the composition?

Impact on Groove: Evaluate how well syncopated rhythms enhance the overall groove and contribute to audience engagement.

Connection with Melody and Harmony:

Rhythmic Harmony: Consider how your rhythmic patterns complement and enhance the melody and harmony. Do they create a cohesive musical experience?

Contrast Analysis: Assess whether rhythmic contrasts with the melody and harmony contribute to a more dynamic listening experience.

Feedback from Audiences:

Live Performances: If possible, gather feedback from live performances. How do audiences respond to different rhythmic elements during a performance?

Online Platforms: Analyze comments and reactions on online platforms where your composition is shared. Look for trends in audience responses.

Collaboration and Collective Engagement:

Collaborative Dynamics: If collaborating with other musicians, consider how the collective rhythmic dynamics contribute to audience engagement. Are there moments of synergy that captivate the listeners?

Interactive Listening: Evaluate how rhythmic interplay between instruments fosters a sense of connection and interactive listening.

Anticipate Audience Movement:

Physical Engagement: Consider how your rhythmic patterns may prompt physical responses from the audience. Are there sections where listeners might naturally tap their feet, clap, or move in sync with the music?

Danceability: If applicable, assess whether the composition's rhythmic patterns make it danceable.

Impact of Breaks and Pauses:

Strategic Breaks: Examine how strategically placed breaks or pauses in your rhythmic patterns contribute to audience engagement. Do these moments create suspense or surprise?

Enhancing Dynamics: Consider whether breaks and pauses enhance the overall dynamic structure of the composition.

Repetition and Catchiness:

Memorability: Assess how repeated rhythmic patterns contribute to the memorability of your composition. Are there rhythmic motifs that stick with the audience?

Catchy Elements: Identify rhythmic elements that make your composition instantly recognizable or catchy.

Dynamic Recording Techniques:

Studio Effects: If recording, explore how studio effects or production techniques enhance the impact of your rhythmic patterns. Does the recording add depth and richness to the overall experience?

Experimentation with Soundscapes: Consider how experimentation with soundscapes and spatial effects contributes to audience engagement.

Consideration of Audience Demographics:

Target Audience: Understand the demographics of your target audience. How might different age groups or cultural backgrounds respond to specific rhythmic patterns?

Adaptability: Be open to adapting rhythmic elements based on the preferences of your intended audience.

Interactive Performance Elements:

Engaging Stage Presence: If performing live, assess how your stage presence and engagement with the audience amplify the impact of your rhythmic patterns.

Visual Coordination: Consider whether visual elements, such as coordinated movements or expressions, enhance the audience's connection with your rhythmic performance.

Storytelling through Rhythm:

Narrative Structure: Explore how rhythmic patterns contribute to the storytelling aspect of your composition. Do they convey a narrative or evoke imagery for the audience?

Emotional Resonance: Assess how specific rhythmic choices align with the emotional journey you want to guide your audience through.

Social Media Analytics:

Online Engagement: Analyze engagement metrics on social media platforms. Which rhythmic patterns generate more likes, shares, or comments? Are there patterns that resonate more with online audiences?

Educational Workshops or Clinics:

Educational Outreach: Conduct workshops or clinics to educate audiences about the rhythmic elements in your composition. How does understanding the rhythm enhance their appreciation of the music?

Q&A Sessions: Engage in Q&A sessions to directly gather insights from audience members about their perception of the rhythmic aspects.

Continuous Evolution:

Feedback Integration: Continuously integrate feedback and insights from audience engagement into your composition. How can you refine or evolve the rhythmic patterns based on audience responses?

Adaptation to Audience Preferences: Stay adaptable and open to making adjustments that align with audience preferences.

By actively considering these aspects and seeking feedback from your audience, you can gain valuable insights into how your rhythmic patterns contribute to audience engagement. This understanding will empower you to refine and tailor your compositions for a more impactful and resonant musical experience.

CROSS-RHYTHMS

Introduce cross-rhythms by juxtaposing different rhythmic patterns in different voices or layers. Cross-rhythms can create a sense of tension and interest.

EXPERIMENTING WITH CROSS-RHYTHMS

Introducing cross-rhythms, also known as polyrhythms, is a fascinating way to add complexity and rhythmic interest to your guitar composition. Polyrhythms involve the simultaneous use of different rhythmic patterns, creating a rich and layered texture.

UNDERSTANDING CROSS-RHYTHMS

Choose Time Signatures:

Start by selecting time signatures for the different layers. Common choices include 3/4, 4/4, 5/4, or 6/8.

Example: Juxtaposing 3/4 in one layer against 4/4 in another.

Establish a Pulse:

Ensure that each layer maintains a clear and consistent pulse. This will help anchor the listener amid the complexity.

Example: Set a steady quarter note pulse in one layer and a triplet pulse in another.

Layering Different Rhythmic Patterns:

Apply contrasting rhythmic patterns to each layer. This can involve using different subdivisions, accents, or syncopations.

Example: Layer a simple quarter-note pattern in one voice with a more intricate pattern involving eighth-note triplets in another.

Maintain Clarity:

Strive for clarity in each layer. While polyrhythms add complexity, it's essential that listeners can still perceive and follow each rhythm.

Example: Keep one layer rhythmically straightforward while the other introduces complexity.

EXAMPLES OF CROSS-RHYTHMS IN GUITAR COMPOSITION

Against 4:

Layer 1 (3/4): Play a repeating pattern of quarter notes in 3/4 time.

Layer 2 (4/4): Simultaneously play a repeating pattern of quarter notes, creating a polyrhythmic effect.

Against 6:

Layer 1 (5/4): Use a rhythmic pattern of quarter notes, eighth notes, and triplets in 5/4 time.

Layer 2 (6/8): Play a contrasting pattern using eighth notes and triplets in 6/8 time.

Against 3:

Layer 1 (2/4): Employ a straightforward eighth-note pattern in 2/4 time.

Layer 2 (3/4): Introduce a contrasting triplet-based pattern in 3/4 time.

Against 8:

Layer 1 (7/8): Create a unique rhythmic motif using a mix of seven eighth notes.

Layer 2 (8/8 or 4/4): Overlay a more conventional rhythm based on eight eighth notes, creating tension and release.

Cross-Rhythmic Strumming:

Layer 1: Strum a chord progression using a consistent 4/4 rhythm.

Layer 2: Introduce cross-rhythmic elements by fingerpicking or arpeggiating a different pattern in 5/4 time.

Syncopated Cross-Rhythms:

Layer 1: Play a syncopated pattern in 4/4 time, emphasizing offbeats.

Layer 2: Introduce a contrasting syncopated pattern in 3/4 time, creating rhythmic tension.

TIPS FOR IMPLEMENTATION

Start Simple:

Begin with straightforward polyrhythms before delving into more complex combinations.

Gradual Introduction:

Introduce cross-rhythms gradually, allowing the listener to acclimate to the layered patterns.

Use Dynamics:

Experiment with dynamic variations between layers to enhance the expressive quality of the polyrhythms.

Experiment with Different Voicings:

Explore various voicings on the guitar to find combinations that allow each layer to stand out.

Combine Cross-Rhythms with Melody:

Integrate cross-rhythms with your melodic lines for a seamless fusion of complexity and musicality.

Experiment with Tempo:

Adjust the tempo to find a balance that enhances the rhythmic complexity without sacrificing clarity.

Practice Methodically:

Practice each layer independently before combining them to ensure precision and mastery.

Record and Listen:

Record your composition and actively listen to identify how the cross-rhythms contribute to the overall texture.

Introducing cross-rhythms adds a sophisticated layer to your guitar composition, creating a sense of rhythmic intrigue and complexity. By carefully selecting time signatures, establishing a pulse, and layering different rhythmic patterns, you can craft a composition that engages and captivates your audience.

INCORPORATE RHYTHMIC MOTIFS

Develop rhythmic motifs that repeat throughout the composition. These motifs can serve as rhythmic anchors, providing continuity and a recognizable rhythmic identity.

DEVELOPING RHYTHMIC MOTIFS

Developing rhythmic motifs that repeat throughout your guitar composition can create cohesion and a sense of familiarity, contributing to a strong and memorable musical identity.

Define the Core Rhythmic Motif:

Choose a Seed Pattern: Begin with a short rhythmic pattern or motif that serves as the core of your idea.

Example:

```

Core Motif: | 1 e & a | 2 e & a |
```


Experiment with Variations:

Subtle Modifications: Explore slight variations to the core motif, altering note lengths, accents, or subdivisions.

Example:

```

Variation 1: | 1 e & a | 2 e & a |
Variation 2: | 1 e & a | 2 e & a |
```

Extend or Shorten Motifs:

Create Length Variations: Extend or shorten the duration of the motifs to add dynamic contrast.

Example:
```

Extended Motif: | 1 e & a | 2 e & a | 3 e & a |
Shortened Motif: | 1 e & a |
```

Introduce Rests:

Silent Spaces: Experiment with the inclusion of rests to create rhythmic tension and allow moments of silence.

Example:
```

Restful Motif: | 1 e & a |   2   | 3 e & a |
```

Polyrhythmic Variations:

Combine with Cross-Rhythms: Layer the rhythmic motif with polyrhythmic variations for complexity.

Example:
```

Polyrhythmic Motif: | 1 e & a | 2 e & a | 3 e & a |
```

Harmonic Embellishments:

Sync with Harmony: Align rhythmic motifs with harmonic changes or embellishments for melodic interest.

Example:
```

Harmonic Embellished Motif: | 1  e  &  a | 2 e & a | 3 e & a |
```


Change in Articulation:

Experiment with Articulation: Vary articulation (legato, staccato, etc.) to impart different expressive qualities.

Example:
```

Legato Motif: | 1  e  &  a | 2 e & a | 3 e & a |
Staccato Motif: | 1 & 2 & 3 & |
```


Incorporate Dynamics:

Dynamic Shaping: Apply dynamic changes to the motifs for expressive impact.

Example:
```

Dynamic Motif: | 1 ff e & a | 2 p e & a | 3 mf e & a |
```

Rhythmic Phrasing in Melody:

Merge with Melody: Integrate rhythmic motifs into the overall melodic structure for a unified composition.

Example:
```
Melodic Motif: | C e & a | D e & a | G e & a |
```

Call-and-Response Techniques:

Create Dialogue: Develop call-and-response patterns between rhythmic motifs for dynamic interaction.

Example:
```
Call: | 1 e & a | 2 e & a |
Response: | 3 e & a | 4 e & a |
```

Explore Odd Time Signatures:

Unconventional Timing: Experiment with odd time signatures to introduce unique rhythmic motifs.

Example:
```
Odd Time Motif: | 1 e & a | 2 e & a | 3 e & a | 4 e & a |
```

Layered Motifs:

Combine Layers: Layer multiple rhythmic motifs simultaneously to create intricate textures.

Example:

```

Layered Motif 1: | 1  e  &  a | 2  e  &  a | 3  e
&  a |
Layered Motif 2: | 1  &  2  &  | 3  e  &  a | 4  e
&  a |

```

Transition Motifs:

Connect Sections: Develop motifs that serve as transitional elements between different sections of your composition.

Example:

```

Transition Motif: | 1  e  &  a | 2  e  &  a | 3 & 4
&  |

```

Pedal Point Motifs:

Sustain a Note: Establish a pedal point or sustained note within the motif for stability.

Example:

```

Pedal Point Motif: | 1  &  2  &  | 3  e  &  a | 4  &
a  |

```

Layering Percussive Elements:

Percussive Texture: Incorporate percussive elements like muted strums or tapping within rhythmic motifs.

Example:
```

Percussive Motif: | 1 & a | 2 e & a | 3 e & a |
```


Tips for Development:

Repetition for Emphasis: Repeated exposure to a rhythmic motif reinforces its significance within the composition.

Combine Multiple Techniques: Experiment with various techniques simultaneously to enrich the complexity of your rhythmic motifs.

Interactive Listening: Actively listen to how rhythmic motifs interact with other elements in your composition to ensure coherence.

Developing rhythmic motifs is a creative process that involves experimentation and exploration. By refining and expanding upon these motifs, you can craft a rhythmic framework that contributes to the overall character and identity of your guitar composition.

SMOOTH TRANSITIONS

Ensure that rhythmic transitions between sections are smooth and well-executed. Consistent rhythmic elements can facilitate seamless transitions.

CREATING SMOOTH TRANSITIONS

Ensuring smooth and well-executed rhythmic transitions between sections in your guitar composition is crucial for maintaining coherence and engaging the listener.

COMMON RHYTHMIC ELEMENT

Bridge Sections with Shared Rhythmic Elements:
Example: If the first section ends with a syncopated rhythm, introduce a similar syncopation at the beginning of the next section.

TRANSITIONAL FILL OR ROLL

Use Percussive or Arpeggiated Fills:
Example: Employ a quick arpeggiated run on the guitar strings or a percussive fill to smoothly connect two sections.

EXTEND FINAL RHYTHMIC PATTERN

Carry Over the Last Rhythm into the Next Section:
Example: If the final measure of Section A ends with a distinctive rhythm, extend that rhythm into the first measure of Section B.

Crossfade or Legato Transition:

Blend Sections with Crossfade or Legato Techniques: Gradually increase the intensity of the strumming or picking to create a crossfade effect between sections.

Common Percussive Element:

Introduce Shared Percussive Hits: Use a snare drum-like percussive hit on the guitar body as a transitional element that repeats in both sections.

Shift in Dynamic Intensity:

Build or Diminish Dynamics for a Gradual Shift: Gradually increase strumming intensity or picking dynamics as you transition from a softer section to a more energetic one.

Use of Grace Notes:

Introduce Grace Notes as Transitional Ornaments: Add quick grace notes leading into the next section to create a sense of anticipation and smoothness.

Seamless Tempo Changes:

Gradual Tempo Shifts for Smooth Transition: If transitioning to a slower section, gradually decrease the tempo in the final measures of the previous section.

Chromatic Walk-Up or Walk-Down:

Chromatic Movement Connecting Sections: Incorporate a short chromatic walk-up or walk-down to bridge the gap between two sections.

Syncopated Hits or Stabs:

Syncopated Chords or Single-Note Hits: Use punctuated, syncopated chord stabs or single-note hits as a rhythmic bridge between sections.

Silent Beat or Rest:

Brief Pause for Dramatic Effect: Insert a brief silence or rest on the final beat of a section before launching into the next, creating a dramatic pause.

Rhythmic Pedal Point:

Sustain a Repeating Note as a Pedal: Hold a sustained note or repeating pattern that serves as a rhythmic pedal point, connecting two contrasting sections.

Contrast in Strumming Patterns:

Shift Strumming Patterns Gradually: If moving from a fingerstyle pattern to strumming, transition by gradually incorporating more strumming in the final measures.

Extend Drum or Percussion Pattern:

Extend Drum or Percussion Elements: Extend a drum fill or percussion pattern from the outro of one section into the introduction of the next.

Common Melodic Rhythmic Motif:

Reprise a Melodic Rhythm as a Link: Reintroduce a melodic rhythm from the previous section as a recurring motif, creating a sense of continuity.

TIPS FOR EXECUTION

Practice Smooth Transitions:
Ensure transitions are practiced and comfortable to execute seamlessly.

Listen Actively:
Actively listen to how the rhythm flows between sections to identify areas that may need adjustment.

Maintain Consistent Tempo:
Keep a consistent tempo throughout the transition to avoid abrupt shifts.

Experiment and Revise:
Experiment with different transition techniques and revise until you achieve the desired smoothness.

By incorporating these techniques and examples into your composition, you can create rhythmic transitions that enhance the flow and cohesiveness of your guitar piece, ensuring a seamless and engaging listening experience.

PLAYING STYLE

Consider your own playing style and comfort with certain rhythmic patterns. Adapt the patterns to showcase your strengths and expressiveness on the guitar.

TAILORING RHYTHMIC PATTERNS

Adapting rhythmic patterns to your playing style is a crucial aspect of creating a guitar composition that feels authentic and resonates with your unique musical voice.

IDENTIFY YOUR PLAYING STYLE

Analyze Your Natural Playing Tendencies:
Example: If you naturally gravitate towards fingerstyle playing, acknowledge this as a defining element of your style.

UNDERSTAND YOUR STRENGTHS

Embrace Your Strengths in Rhythmic Execution:
Example: If you excel at percussive strumming, incorporate rhythmic patterns that highlight this strength.

ANALYZE YOUR INFLUENCES

Consider Influences on Your Playing:
Example: If you are influenced by blues, infuse rhythmic patterns reminiscent of blues guitarists into your composition.

Start with Patterns You're Comfortable With:

Example: Begin by incorporating rhythmic patterns you often use in your improvisations or favorite songs.

Highlight Distinctive Phrasing Techniques:

Example: If you have a penchant for sliding between notes, integrate slides into your rhythmic patterns.

Modify Patterns Based on Your Picking Style:

Example: If you prefer alternate picking, adapt rhythmic patterns to suit the fluidity of this technique.

Bring in Personal Articulation Techniques:

Example: If you often use hammer-ons and pull-offs, embed them within your rhythmic patterns for added flair.

Tailor Strumming to Your Strumming Hand Habits:

Example: Adjust strumming patterns to align with the natural motion of your strumming hand.

Integrate Hybrid Picking Techniques:

Example: If hybrid picking is part of your playing style, experiment with rhythmic patterns that leverage this technique.

Modify Density Based on Your Comfort Level:

Example: If intricate picking patterns suit you, introduce sections with higher rhythmic density.

Express Emotion Through Rhythm:

Example: Use rhythmic patterns that resonate with the emotional tone you want to convey, aligning with your natural expression.

Explore Fingerstyle Techniques:

Example: Fingerstyle players can experiment with arpeggiated patterns or thumb-slaps to create rhythmic interest.

Incorporate Open Strings to Enhance Your Style:

Example: If you appreciate the resonance of open strings, design patterns that make use of open notes.

Adjust Syncopation to Suit Your Taste:

Example: If you enjoy syncopated rhythms, tailor them to align with your preferred offbeat accents.

TIPS FOR ADAPTATION

Experimentation is Key:

Continuously experiment with different rhythmic patterns to discover what feels most natural to you.

Listen to Your Own Playing:

Actively listen to recordings of your playing to identify recurring rhythmic tendencies.

Modify Existing Patterns:

Take existing rhythmic patterns and modify them to incorporate elements of your playing style.

Blend Techniques Smoothly:

Seamlessly blend different techniques within your rhythmic patterns to create a cohesive sound.

Adapting rhythmic patterns to your playing style involves a deep understanding of your strengths, preferences, and influences. By incorporating your unique phrasing, articulation, and techniques into rhythmic patterns, you can create a composition that authentically represents your musical identity. Remember, the goal is not to conform to a particular style but to showcase your individuality as a guitarist.

Rhythm is a powerful tool for shaping the character and impact of your guitar composition. Whether you're aiming for a driving, energetic rhythm or a subtle, contemplative feel, thoughtful consideration and experimentation with rhythmic patterns will contribute significantly to the success of your musical creation.

TIME SIGNATURE

Experiment with different time signatures to add rhythmic interest.

EXPERIMENTING WITH TIME SIGNATURES

Experimenting with different time signatures is a great way to add rhythmic interest and complexity to your guitar compositions. Time signatures influence the rhythmic structure of your music, and exploring various meters can lead to unique and compelling rhythmic patterns.

UNDERSTAND TIME SIGNATURES

Understanding time signatures is essential for effective rhythm and timing in guitar composition. Time signatures indicate the organization of beats within a measure, providing a framework for your musical ideas.

Let's get into more detail to help you comprehend and utilize time signatures in your guitar compositions.

Time Signature Notation:
Time signatures are typically written as a fraction at the beginning of a musical piece. The top number denotes the number of beats in a measure, while the bottom number indicates the note value that represents one beat.

COMMON TIME SIGNATURES

4/4 Time Signature:

Four quarter-note beats per measure. Most common and versatile.

3/4 Time Signature:

Three quarter-note beats per measure. Often associated with waltz rhythms.

6/8 Time Signature:

Six eighth-note beats per measure. Common in compound meters, creating a feel of two groups of three.

UNDERSTANDING THE TOP NUMBER

Number of Beats:

The top number indicates how many beats are in each measure.

Example: In 4/4, there are four beats in each measure.

UNDERSTANDING THE BOTTOM NUMBER

Note Value for a Beat:

The bottom number represents the note value that receives one beat.

Example: In 4/4, the quarter note receives one beat.

Simple vs. Compound Meters:

Simple Meters: Beats are divided into two.

Examples: 2/4, 3/4, 4/4.

Compound Meters: Beats are divided into three.

Examples: 6/8, 9/8, 12/8.

PRACTICAL APPLICATION FOR GUITARISTS

Strumming Patterns:

Adjust strumming patterns based on the number of beats in a measure.

Example: In 3/4, strumming down on beats 1 and 2, and up on beat 3 creates a natural waltz feel.

Emphasize Strong Beats:

Accentuate the first beat in each measure for clarity and rhythm.

Example: In 4/4, accentuate beats 1 and 3.

Dynamic Shifts:

Changing time signatures can introduce a dynamic shift in your composition.

Example: Shifting from 4/4 to 6/8 can alter the feel and create interest.

Playing Off the Beat:

Experiment with syncopated rhythms for off-beat accents.

Example: In 4/4, emphasize the "and" of each beat for a syncopated feel.

Layering Different Meters:

Experiment with polyrhythms by layering different time signatures.

Example: Overlaying 3/4 against 4/4 creates a polyrhythmic effect.

Use a Metronome:

Practice with a metronome to develop a solid sense of timing.

Example: Set the metronome to the desired beats per minute (BPM) for consistent practice.

Rock and Pop:

Many rock and pop songs use 4/4 time for its straightforward feel.

Jazz and Blues:

Jazz and blues may explore different meters, adding complexity and variety.

TIPS FOR MASTERY

Start Simple:

Begin with common time signatures before exploring more complex ones.

Listen Actively:

Pay attention to time signatures in your favorite songs to understand their impact.

Understanding time signatures is an integral part of becoming a proficient guitarist and composer. As you experiment with different time signatures, you'll gain greater control over the rhythmic aspects of your compositions, allowing for creative expression and musical diversity.

COMMON TIME SIGNATURE EXAMPLES

Begin by experimenting with common time signatures like 4/4, 3/4, and 6/8. These signatures provide a solid foundation and are widely used in various musical genres.

Below we dive into common and less common time signatures with examples.

COMMON TIME SIGNATURES

4/4 Time Signature:

Description: Four quarter-note beats per measure.

Example: Common in rock, pop, and most contemporary music.

3/4 Time Signature:

Description: Three quarter-note beats per measure.
Example: Often used in waltzes and ballads.

6/8 Time Signature:

Description: Six eighth-note beats per measure, grouped into two sets of three.

Example: Common in compound meters, creating a feel of two groups of three.

2/4 Time Signature:

Description: Two quarter-note beats per measure.
Example: Found in many marches and fast-paced music.

5/4 Time Signature:

Description: Five quarter-note beats per measure.

Example: Used for asymmetrical or progressive feels.

7/8 Time Signature:

Description: Seven eighth-note beats per measure, often grouped as 2+2+3.

Example: Common in progressive rock and world music.

EXPERIMENTING WITH COMMON TIME SIGNATURES

Create a 7/8 Groove:

Example:

Strum a repeating pattern emphasizing 2+2+3 accents. Experiment with variations in picking and strumming patterns.

Mix 4/4 and 6/8:

Example:

Start with a 4/4 verse and transition to a 6/8 chorus for a dynamic shift. Explore how it alters the feel of the composition.

Use 3/4 for Ballad Sections:

Example:

Employ 3/4 time for introspective or ballad sections, allowing for a softer, more flowing feel.

Experiment with 5/4 Riffs:

Example:

Create a distinctive guitar riff using a 5/4 time signature. This can add an intriguing, slightly irregular character to your composition.

Layer 6/8 with 4/4:

Example:

Overlay a 6/8 rhythm on one guitar track while maintaining a 4/4 rhythm on another. This creates polyrhythmic textures.

Shift Between 3/4 and 4/4:

Example:

Transition between 3/4 and 4/4 within a composition. This can create a sense of unpredictability and interest.

Experiment with 2/4 in Upbeat Sections:

Example:

Use 2/4 in energetic, upbeat sections to give the composition a brisk and lively feel.

Create a 5/4 Drum Pattern:

Example:

Coordinate a drum pattern in 5/4, and build guitar elements around this unconventional rhythmic foundation.

Combine 7/8 with Syncopation:

Example:

Introduce syncopated elements within a 7/8 time signature to add complexity and rhythmic interest.

Explore 9/8 for Progressive Feel:

Example:

Use 9/8 in progressive sections for a slightly odd time feel, allowing for intricate guitar work.

TIPS FOR EXPERIMENTATION

Start Simple:

Begin experimenting with common time signatures before delving into more complex ones.

Listen Actively:

Analyze songs in different time signatures to understand how they contribute to the overall feel.

Blend with Familiar Elements:

Combine unconventional time signatures with familiar chord progressions or melodic motifs to maintain listener engagement.

Experimenting with different time signatures can open up new possibilities for your guitar compositions, allowing you to craft unique and captivating musical experiences. As you explore, keep in mind the emotional and rhythmic impact each time signature brings to your composition.

UNCOMMON TIME SIGNATURE EXAMPLES

Dive into less common time signatures such as 5/4, 7/8, 9/8, or even more complex meters like 11/16. Uncommon time signatures can add a unique rhythmic flair to your composition.

Exploring uncommon time signatures in guitar composition can add a distinctive and innovative touch to your music. Uncommon time signatures go beyond the standard 4/4 or 3/4, offering a unique rhythmic palette.

Understand Uncommon Time Signatures

Definition: Uncommon time signatures deviate from the traditional 4/4, 3/4, or 6/8 and may involve odd or prime numbers of beats per measure.

EXAMPLES OF UNCOMMON TIME SIGNATURES

5/4:

Five quarter-note beats per measure.
Example:
Dave Brubeck's *Take Five* features a famous 5/4 jazz groove.

7/8:

Seven eighth-note beats per measure, often grouped as 3+4 or 4+3.
Example:
Pink Floyd's *Money* employs a recurring 7/8 time signature.

9/8:

Nine eighth-note beats per measure, often grouped as 3+3+3.

Example:

Solsbury Hill by Peter Gabriel has sections in 9/8.

11/8:

Eleven eighth-note beats per measure, often grouped as 3+3+3+2.

Example:

Schism by Tool features passages in 11/8.

13/8:

Thirteen eighth-note beats per measure, often grouped as 3+3+3+2+2.

Example:

Blue Rondo à la Turk by Dave Brubeck blends 9/8 and 5/4 sections.

EXPERIMENTATION WITH UNCOMMON TIME SIGNATURES

Mix Odd and Even Signatures:

Example:

Transition from 7/8 to 4/4 for a dynamic and unexpected shift.

Polyrhythmic Sections:

Example:

Overlap a 5/4 guitar riff with a 6/8 drum pattern to create polyrhythmic complexity.

Time Signature Changes:

Example:

Shift between 7/8 and 5/4 to add unpredictability and interest.

Contrast with Common Signatures:

Example:

Pair an uncommon time signature like 11/8 with a section in 4/4 for contrast.

Harmonic Rhythmic Alignment:

Example:

Align chord changes with specific beats in uncommon time signatures for harmonic rhythmic coherence.

USE OF UNCOMMON SIGNATURES IN DIFFERENT GENRES

Progressive Rock/Metal:

Uncommon time signatures are prevalent, adding complexity and sophistication.

Example:

Dream Theater frequently uses irregular time signatures in their compositions.

Jazz:

Jazz often incorporates odd meters for improvisational exploration.

Example:

John Coltrane's *Giant Steps* includes sections in 9/8.

World Music:

Many world music genres embrace unique rhythmic structures.

Example:

African and Indian music often feature irregular time signatures.

TIPS FOR EFFECTIVE USE

Complement the Composition:

Ensure that the chosen time signature enhances rather than distracts from the overall musical narrative.

Maintain Groove:

Even in uncommon time signatures, aim to maintain a sense of groove and rhythm.

Gradual Introduction:

If incorporating unconventional signatures, introduce them gradually to ease listener assimilation.

Embrace Experimentation:

Don't be afraid to experiment with less common meters to discover new and exciting rhythmic possibilities.

Push Boundaries:

Uncommon time signatures challenge traditional rhythmic norms, fostering creative exploration.

Develop Unique Soundscapes:

Use uncommon signatures to create compositions with a distinct and memorable rhythmic identity.

Exploring uncommon time signatures in guitar composition is a journey into uncharted rhythmic territories. By understanding their characteristics, experimenting with their application, and drawing inspiration from diverse genres, you can craft compositions that stand out with inventive and captivating rhythms. Remember, the key is to use these signatures purposefully to enhance your musical expression.

MIXED OR COMPOUND SIGNATURES

Experiment with mixed or compound time signatures, combining, for example, simple and compound meters within a single composition. This adds layers of rhythmic complexity.

INCORPORATING MIXED OR COMPOUND SIGNATURES

Mixed or compound time signatures add a layer of complexity and intrigue to your guitar compositions by combining elements of both simple and compound meters.

Definition:

Mixed or compound time signatures combine elements of simple and compound meters within the same measure.

EXAMPLES OF MIXED OR COMPOUND TIME SIGNATURES

7/8:
- Seven eighth-note beats per measure.
- Can be considered mixed due to its odd grouping.

Example: *Money* by Pink Floyd.

5/4:
- Five quarter-note beats per measure.
- Mixes elements of simple and compound rhythms.

Example: *Take Five* by Dave Brubeck.

11/8:

- Eleven eighth-note beats per measure, often grouped as 3+3+3+2.
- Combines elements of compound and asymmetrical rhythms.

Example: *Schism* by Tool.

INCORPORATING MIXED OR COMPOUND SIGNATURES

Polyrhythmic Patterns:

Example:

Introduce a polyrhythmic section where one guitar plays in 4/4 while another plays in 7/8, creating rhythmic tension.

Shifting Accents:

Example:

Shift accents within a measure, emphasizing different parts of a mixed signature for dynamic phrasing.

Alternating Sections:

Example:

Switch between sections in 4/4 and 6/8 to create contrast and maintain listener engagement.

Layering Simple and Compound Rhythms:

Example:

Layer a compound rhythm in the drums with a simple rhythm in the guitar, creating intricate rhythmic textures.

Emphasizing Specific Beats:

Example:

Emphasize specific beats within a compound signature to create a unique groove while maintaining a straightforward feel.

BENEFITS OF MIXED OR COMPOUND SIGNATURES

Rich Rhythmic Texture:

Mixed signatures provide a nuanced rhythmic texture that can elevate your composition.

Experimental Soundscapes:

They open doors to experimental soundscapes by combining contrasting rhythmic elements.

Dynamic Expressiveness:

Mixed signatures allow for dynamic expressiveness, offering both complexity and clarity.

TIPS FOR INCORPORATION

Gradual Introduction:

Example:

Introduce mixed signatures gradually within your composition to allow listeners to acclimate.

Cohesive Transitions:

Example:

Ensure smooth transitions between sections with mixed signatures to maintain overall coherence

Harmonic Alignment:

Example:

Align chord changes with specific beats in mixed signatures to enhance harmonic rhythmic cohesion.

Experiment with Different Ratios:

Example:

Explore different ratios in mixed signatures to discover unique rhythmic patterns.

APPLICATION ACROSS GENRES

Fusion and Jazz-Rock:

Mixed signatures are common in fusion and jazz-rock, allowing for intricate rhythmic interplay.

Example:

Mahavishnu Orchestra's *Birds of Fire* features mixed meters.

Progressive Metal:

Progressive metal often utilizes mixed signatures to create complex and dynamic rhythms.

Example:

Between the Buried and Me's *Selkies: The Endless Obsession* incorporates mixed meters.

World Music Influences:

World music genres frequently incorporate mixed signatures for cultural rhythmic diversity.

Example:

South Indian classical music often features mixed meters.

Create Unique Grooves:

Example:

Experiment with mixed signatures to forge distinctive grooves that set your composition apart.

Dynamic Rhythmic Pacing:

Example:

Utilize mixed signatures to control the rhythmic pacing of your composition dynamically.

Mixed or compound time signatures offer a realm of creative possibilities in guitar composition. Whether you're aiming for intricate polyrhythmic textures, experimental soundscapes, or dynamic expressiveness, integrating mixed signatures can elevate your rhythmic patterns and bring a unique character to your music. Embrace experimentation, and let the rhythmic complexity of mixed signatures enhance the rhythmic landscape of your guitar compositions.

TIME SIGNATURE AND PHRASING

Align your choice of time signatures with the phrasing of your melody or thematic material. This connection enhances the rhythmic coherence between different musical elements.

ALIGNING TIME SIGNATURE WITH PHRASING

Aligning your choice of time signatures with the phrasing of your melody or thematic material is crucial for creating a harmonious and cohesive musical experience in guitar composition.

Understanding Melodic Phrasing:
Definition: Melodic phrasing refers to the rhythmic and melodic structure of a musical idea, often characterized by the arrangement of notes and their durations.

Importance of Alignment:
Aligning time signatures with melodic phrasing ensures a seamless integration of rhythm and melody, enhancing the overall musical coherence.

EXAMPLES OF ALIGNMENT

4/4 Time Signature with Regular Phrasing:
Example:
If your melody has a straightforward and regular phrasing, using a common time signature like 4/4 can provide a stable and familiar rhythmic foundation.

3/4 Time Signature for Waltz-like Phrasing:

Example:

If your melody has a waltz-like phrasing, where accents fall on the first beat of each measure, using 3/4 time signature can enhance the graceful and flowing quality.

7/8 Time Signature for Complex Phrasing:

Example:

If your melody features intricate and asymmetrical phrasing, using an odd time signature like 7/8 can complement the complexity, creating an engaging rhythmic interplay.

Alternating Signatures for Varied Phrasing:

Example:

For a melody with sections of varied phrasing, consider alternating between time signatures to accentuate different rhythmic nuances.

Syncopated Melody with Syncopated Signatures:

Example:

If your melody incorporates syncopation or offbeat accents, choosing time signatures with syncopated patterns (e.g., 7/8 or 9/8) can enhance the rhythmic syncopation.

TIPS FOR ALIGNMENT

Analyze Melodic Accents:

Example:

Identify the accented notes in your melody and choose time signatures that emphasize these accents for rhythmic clarity.

Complement Phrasing Dynamics:

Example:

Match the dynamic shifts and articulations in your melody with appropriate time signature changes for expressive cohesion.

Seamless Transitions:

Example:

Ensure smooth transitions between different sections with varying time signatures to maintain overall coherence.

Experiment with Ratios:

Example:

Experiment with time signature ratios to align rhythmic patterns with the duration and emphasis of melodic phrases.

APPLICATION ACROSS GENRES

Jazz Standards:

Jazz compositions often align time signatures with the intricate phrasing of improvisational melodies.

Example:

John Coltrane's *Giant Steps* features a challenging 3/4 and 4/4 alternation, aligning with the complex melodic lines.

Progressive Rock/Metal:

Progressive genres frequently align time signatures with the intricate phrasing of progressive melodic elements.

Example:

Dream Theater's *Dance of Eternity* showcases intricate melodic phrasing aligned with changing time signatures.

Folk Music:

Folk compositions often align time signatures with the natural phrasing of folk melodies.

Example:

Scarborough Fair features a 3/4 time signature, complementing the flowing nature of the melody.

Create Dynamic Rhythmic Palettes:

Example:

Experiment with different time signatures to create dynamic rhythmic palettes that enhance the emotional and expressive qualities of your melody.

Harmonic Rhythmic Resonance:

Example:

Align the harmonic progressions with the rhythmic pulses of the melody, creating a resonant connection between harmony and rhythm.

Aligning time signatures with the phrasing of your melody adds depth and sophistication to your guitar composition. The key is to carefully consider the rhythmic characteristics of your melody and choose time signatures that complement and enhance those characteristics. Experimentation and a keen ear for rhythmic nuances will guide you towards achieving a seamless integration of time signatures and melodic phrasing in your guitar compositions.

CHANGING TIME SIGNATURES

Introduce dynamic changes by incorporating sections with changing time signatures. Gradual or abrupt shifts in meter can create moments of tension, surprise, or resolution.

USING CHANGING TIME SIGNATURES

Introducing dynamic changes through the incorporation of sections with changing time signatures is a powerful technique in guitar composition. This approach adds excitement, complexity, and a sense of progression to your music.

Understanding Changing Time Signatures:

Changing time signatures involve transitioning between different rhythmic patterns within a composition, providing diversity in the musical structure.

Benefits of Changing Time Signatures:

Example:

Shifting from 4/4 to 7/8 can create tension, excitement, and a sense of unpredictability.

GENRE EXAMPLES

Jazz Fusion:

Example:

Chick Corea's *Spain* introduces sections with changing time signatures, contributing to the dynamic nature of the composition.

Classical Influence:

Example:

Stravinsky's *Rite of Spring* incorporates shifting time signatures to create rhythmic complexity and intensity.

HOW TO INTRODUCE DYNAMIC CHANGES

Compose Transitional Passages:

Example:

Craft sections that serve as transitional passages, guiding listeners smoothly from one time signature to another.

Build Momentum:

Example:

Use changing time signatures to build momentum towards climactic points in your composition, enhancing the overall dynamic structure.

Vary Time Signature Density:

Example:

Introduce denser time signatures (e.g., 7/8 or 5/4) after sections with simpler signatures to create contrast and interest.

Align with Theme Changes:

Example:

Change time signatures in conjunction with shifts in themes or moods within your composition, reinforcing the emotional impact.

TIPS FOR EFFECTIVE USE

Ensure Seamless Transitions:

Example:

Use rhythmic and melodic motifs that span time signature changes, ensuring seamless transitions for the listener.

Experiment with Syncopation:

Example:

Experiment with syncopated rhythms during transitions to add flair and maintain listener engagement.

Balance Complexity:

Example:

Strike a balance between complex and straightforward time signatures to maintain accessibility while adding depth.

Metal and Djent:

Example:

Bands like Meshuggah frequently use changing time signatures to achieve a djent-style rhythmic complexity.

Progressive Rock:

Example:

Tool's *Schism* features sections with alternating time signatures, contributing to its progressive and intricate feel.

Fusion and Jazz:

Example:

Miles Davis' *Milestones* shifts between time signatures to showcase the versatility of jazz fusion.

Odd Time Signatures:

Example:

Experiment with odd time signatures (e.g., 9/8 or 11/8) to add an extra layer of complexity and intrigue.

Unconventional Pairings:

Example:

Pair unconventional time signatures together (e.g., alternating between 5/4 and 7/8) for a unique rhythmic landscape.

Changing time signatures in your guitar composition allows you to break free from conventional rhythmic structures, providing a canvas for creativity and expression. Whether you're inspired by progressive rock's technical intricacies, jazz's improvisational nature, or classical compositions' rhythmic complexity, incorporating changing time signatures adds a dynamic and captivating dimension to your music. Use this technique strategically to enhance the overall impact of your guitar compositions and keep your audience engaged.

ODD AND PRIME NUMBERS

Delve into time signatures with odd or prime numbers. These signatures, like 7/8 or 11/16, introduce asymmetry and unconventional rhythmic groupings.

EXPLORING ODD AND PRIME NUMBERS

Time signatures with odd or prime numbers add an interesting rhythmic complexity to guitar compositions, breaking away from the more conventional duple or quadruple meter. These time signatures can create a unique and dynamic feel, challenging both the listener and the guitarist.

5/4 Time Signature:

One of the most commonly used odd meters in guitar compositions is 5/4. It has five beats per measure, and it's often counted as "1-2-3-4-5." A classic example is "Take Five" by Dave Brubeck. A guitar piece in 5/4 can have a distinct, asymmetrical groove, providing a sense of tension and anticipation.

Example:
```
e|-------------------|------------------|
B|-------1---3---1-----|-------1---3---1-----|
G|-----2---2---2---2---|-----2---2---2---2---|
D|---3-------------3-|---3-------------3-|
A|-3------------------|-3------------------|
E|-------------------|------------------|
```

7/8 Time Signature:

Moving into prime numbers, 7/8 time signature consists of seven eighth-note beats per measure. This creates a unique rhythmic pattern that can be subdivided into different groupings like 2+2+3 or 3+2+2.

Example:
```
e|-----------------|-----------------|
B|-----1---2---1-----|-----1---2---1-----|
G|---2---2---2---2---|---2---2---2---2---|
D|-2-------------2-|-2-------------2-|
A|-----------------|-----------------|
E|-----------------|-----------------|
```

11/8 Time Signature:

A less common but intriguing time signature is 11/8. This signature consists of eleven eighth-note beats per measure and can be subdivided in various ways, such as 3+3+2+3 or 4+4+3.

Example:

```
```

```
e|-----------------|-----------------|
B|-----1---2---1-----|-----1---2---1-----|
G|---2---2---2---2---|---2---2---2---2---|
D|-2-------------2-|-2-------------2-|
A|-----------------|-----------------|
E|-----------------|-----------------|
```

```
```

When using odd or prime time signatures in guitar compositions, it's crucial to maintain a sense of musicality and flow. Experiment with different rhythmic patterns and accents to create engaging and dynamic pieces that stand out from more conventional compositions.

DUPLE AND TRIPLE METERS

Mix duple (even) and triple (odd) meters within a composition. Alternating between 4/4 and 3/4, for instance, can create a dynamic push and pull effect.

MIXING DUPLE AND TRIPLE METERS

Mixing duple (even) and triple (odd) meters within a guitar composition can add complexity and interest to the rhythmic structure. This fusion creates a dynamic interplay between the steady pulse of even meters and the more irregular feel of odd meters.

Alternating Sections:

Divide your composition into distinct sections with different time signatures. For example, alternate between 4/4 (duple) and 3/4 (triple) meters. This creates a clear contrast between the regular and irregular rhythms.

Example:
```

Section A: | 4/4      | 4/4      | 4/4      | 4/4      |
Section B: | 3/4      | 3/4      | 3/4      | 3/4      |

```

Metric Modulation:

Transition smoothly between duple and triple meters by using a technique known as metric modulation. This involves establishing a new tempo or pulse within the context of the existing meter.

Example:
```

e|----------------|----------------|----------------|
B|-----1---2---1-----|-----1---2---1-----|-----1---2---1-----|
G|---2---2---2---2---|---2---2---2---2---|---2---2---2---2--
-|
D|-2-------------2-|-2-------------2-|-2-------------2-|
 A|----------------|----------------|----------------|
E|----------------|----------------|----------------|
```

Polyrhythms:

Combine different rhythmic patterns simultaneously. For instance, play a melody in 4/4 while the underlying chords follow a 3/4 pattern. This creates a sense of tension and complexity.

Example:
```

Melody: | 1  2  3  4  | 1  2  3  4  | 1  2  3  4  |
Chords: | 1  2  3     | 1  2  3     | 1  2  3     |
```

Syncopation:

Introduce syncopated rhythms within a duple meter. This involves placing accents or emphasizing off-beats, creating a subtle shift toward a triple feel without changing the time signature.

Example:

```
e|----------------|----------------|----------------|
B|-----1-------1-----|-----1-------1-----|-----1-------1-----|
G|---2---2---2---2---|---2---2---2---2---|---2---2---2---2---|
D|-2-------2-------2-|-2-------2-------2-|-2-------2-------2-|
A|----------------|----------------|----------------|
E|----------------|----------------|----------------|
```

Mixed Meter:

Combine both duple and triple subdivisions within the same measure. For example, alternate between 6/8 and 4/4 patterns within a single phrase.

Example:

```
e|--------------------|--------------------|
B|-----1---2---1---2-----|-----1---2---1--2-----|
G|---2---2---2---2---2---|---2---2---2--2--2---|
D|-2------------------|-2------------------|
A|--------------------|--------------------|
E|--------------------|--------------------|
```

Experimenting with these techniques allows you to create guitar compositions that are rhythmically rich and engaging. The key is to maintain a sense of cohesion and musicality while exploring the interplay between duple and triple meters.

OFFBEAT ACCENTS

Play with offbeat accents within the chosen time signature. Shifting accents to offbeats can add syncopation and unexpected rhythmic twists.

EXPERIMENTING WITH OFFBEAT ACCENTS

Offbeat accents involve placing emphasis or emphasis on beats that fall between the regular strong beats of a musical measure. In most Western music, the strong beats are typically on beats 1 and 3 in a 4/4 time signature, and offbeat accents can occur on beats 2 and 4, or any other subdivision of the beat. Incorporating offbeat accents into guitar composition can add rhythmic interest, syncopation, and a sense of groove.

Understanding Offbeat Accents:

Strong beats are usually where you would naturally tap your foot. Offbeat accents occur on the weaker parts of the beat, creating a rhythmic tension that adds excitement and energy to the music.

Incorporating Offbeat Accents:

Use the picking hand (strumming or picking) to accentuate the offbeats. This can involve playing certain notes louder, using a different picking technique, or muting certain beats to create a percussive effect.

Example 1: Simple Offbeat Accents in a Strumming Pattern (4/4 Time Signature):

```
| 1  2  3  4  | 1  2  3  4  | 1  2  3  4  | 1  2  3
4  |
| D  D  D  dU | D  D  D  dU | D  D  D  dU | D
D  D  dU |
```

(D: Downstroke, U: Upstroke)

In this example, the offbeat accents occur on the "and" of each beat, creating a lively and syncopated strumming pattern.

Example 2: Offbeat Accents in a Melodic Phrase (6/8 Time Signature):

```
| 1  2  3  4  5  6  | 1  2  3  4  5  6  | 1  2  3  4
5  6  |
| G  D  A  | G  D  A  | G  D  A  |
```

In this example, the offbeat accents occur between the strong beats in a 6/8 time signature. The dashes represent notes played on the offbeats.

Example 3: Offbeat Accents in a Riff (4/4 Time Signature):

```
e|-----------------|-----------------|-----------------|-----------------|
B|-----------------|-----------------|-----------------|-----------------|
G|-----------------|-----------------|-----------------|-----------------|
D|---5---5---7---7---|---5---5---7---7---|---5---5---7---7---|---5---5---7---7---|
A|-5---5---5---5-----|-5---5---5---5-----|-5---5---5---5-----|-5---5---5---5-----|
E|-----------------|-----------------|-----------------|-----------------|
```

In this example, the accents are placed on the offbeats, giving the riff a rhythmic drive and punch.

Experimentation:

Feel free to experiment with different accent patterns and placements. You can vary the dynamics, add rests, or experiment with different articulations to create a unique rhythmic feel.

By incorporating offbeat accents into your guitar compositions, you can enhance the rhythmic complexity and make your music more engaging and exciting. It's a versatile technique that works well in various genres, from rock and jazz to folk and beyond.

SIMPLE AND COMPOUND RHYTHMS

Combine simple rhythms with compound rhythms. For example, pair a basic 4/4 strumming pattern with a melody featuring compound meter for a layered rhythmic effect.

COMBINING SIMPLE AND COMPOUND RHYTHMS

Combining simple rhythms with compound rhythms in guitar composition adds depth and complexity to your music. Simple rhythms typically involve straightforward divisions of the beat (e.g., quarter notes, eighth notes), while compound rhythms incorporate more intricate subdivisions (e.g., triplets, sixteenth-note triplets). By skillfully integrating these two types of rhythms, you can create interesting and dynamic compositions.

UNDERSTANDING SIMPLE AND COMPOUND RHYTHMS

Simple Rhythms:

These rhythms are based on basic subdivisions, such as quarter notes, eighth notes, and sixteenth notes. They provide a steady and predictable pulse.

Compound Rhythms:

These rhythms involve more complex subdivisions, often in groupings of three (e.g., triplets, sextuplets). They add a sense of fluidity and variation.

Incorporating Simple Rhythms:

Use simple rhythms to establish a foundational groove or pulse. This provides a stable framework for your composition.

Incorporating Compound Rhythms:

Introduce compound rhythms to add intricacy and movement. These can be used to create syncopation, offbeat accents, or polyrhythmic elements.

Example 1: Simple and Compound Rhythms in Strumming (4/4 Time Signature):

```
|1 2 3 4 |1 2 3 4 |1 2 3 4 |1 2 3 4 |
|D UD UD |D UD UD |D UD UD |D UD UD |
```

In this strumming pattern, the downstrokes (D) represent a simple rhythm, while the upstrokes (U) introduce a compound feel. This combination adds both stability and complexity.

Example 2: Simple and Compound Rhythms in a Melodic Phrase (6/8 Time Signature):

```
|1 2 3 4 5 6 |1 2 3 4 5 6 |1 2 3 4 5 6 |
|C  G  A  |C  G  A  |C  G  A  |
```

In this example, a simple melodic phrase in 6/8 time incorporates compound rhythms. The notes on the strong beats are simple, while the notes on the offbeats introduce a compound feel.

Example 3: Simple and Compound Rhythms in a Riff (4/4 Time Signature):

```
e|------------------|------------------|------------------|------------------|
B|------------------|------------------|------------------|------------------|
G|---5---5---7---7---|---5---5---7---7---|---5---5---7---7---|---5---5---7---7---|
D|-5---5---5---5-----|-5---5---5---5-----|-5---5---5---5-----|-5---5---5---5-----|
```

This riff combines simple power chords with a compound feel by using eighth notes and quarter-note triplets. The result is a rhythmic interplay between stability and complexity.

Transitions:

Smoothly transition between simple and compound rhythms to maintain a coherent flow. Gradual changes can be more effective than abrupt shifts.

Experimentation:

Experiment with different combinations and placements of simple and compound rhythms. You can create interesting variations by altering the durations of notes, rests, and accents.

By skillfully combining simple and compound rhythms in your guitar composition, you can craft music that is both rhythmically engaging and musically rich. This approach provides a versatile toolkit for expressing a wide range of emotions and styles within your compositions.

DRUM PATTERNS AND GUITAR RHYTHMS

If working with a drummer or percussionist, align guitar rhythms with complementary drum patterns. This coordination enhances the rhythmic interplay within the ensemble.

ALIGNING DRUM PATTERNS WITH GUITAR RHYTHMS

Aligning drum patterns with guitar rhythms is crucial for creating a cohesive and tight sound in your compositions. The interaction between the guitar and drums forms the backbone of many musical genres, providing the foundation for the overall groove.

Establish a Solid Foundation:

Define the Tempo: Before creating your drum pattern, establish the tempo of your composition. This sets the foundation for both the guitar and drum parts.

Understand the Time Signature: Know the time signature of your composition (e.g., 4/4, 6/8). This helps in organizing rhythmic patterns for both the guitar and drums.

Create a Drum Groove That Complements the Guitar Rhythm:

Coordinate Kick and Snare with Guitar Accents: Align the kick drum hits with the downbeats or strong accents of the guitar, while the snare drum can complement the upbeats or syncopated accents.

Use Tom-Toms for Fills and Transitions: Integrate tom-tom hits in the drum pattern to accentuate transitions, fills, or specific guitar licks. This adds dynamic movement to the composition.

Syncopation and Offbeat Accents: Experiment with drum patterns that include syncopated and offbeat elements, aligning with the guitar's rhythmic intricacies.

Coordinate Hi-Hats and Cymbals:

Hi-Hat Openings/Closings: Use the hi-hat to enhance the dynamic range. For instance, open the hi-hat during guitar choruses or louder sections and close it for softer parts.

Cymbal Crashes: Coordinate cymbal crashes with significant moments in the guitar composition, such as the beginning of a new section or a powerful guitar riff.

Syncopation and Rhythmic Variations:

Introduce Drum Fills: Align drum fills with pauses or breaks in the guitar rhythm. This helps in transitioning between different sections of your composition.

Emphasize Guitar Riffs: Use drum patterns to emphasize and complement specific guitar riffs. This alignment enhances the overall impact of the musical arrangement.

Consistency Across Sections:

Maintain Consistent Groove: Ensure that the drum pattern maintains a consistent groove that complements the overall feel of the guitar composition, even when the dynamics or intensity change.

Communication with Drummer:

Collaborate with Drummer: If you are working with a drummer, communicate your ideas and preferences. Collaborative discussions can lead to a more cohesive and synchronized performance.

Experiment and Fine-Tune:

Try Different Patterns: Experiment with various drum patterns to find the one that best enhances the guitar composition. Small adjustments can have a significant impact on the overall feel.

Listen Critically: Regularly listen to the interplay between the guitar and drums. Make adjustments as needed to maintain a tight and synchronized sound.

Aligning drum patterns with guitar rhythms requires careful consideration of timing, dynamics, and the overall feel of the composition. Through experimentation and collaboration, you can create a rhythmic foundation that enhances the impact and cohesiveness of your guitar-driven music.

METRIC MODULATION

Explore metric modulation, where the tempo remains constant, but the subdivision or pulse changes. This technique can create seamless transitions between different time signatures.

EXPERIMENTING WITH METRIC MODULATION

Metric modulation is a musical technique where the tempo (or pulse) of a piece of music is changed by using a new rhythmic value as a reference. This means that the underlying pulse remains constant, but the subdivision or beat grouping changes, creating a sense of modulation in the perceived tempo. Metric modulation is a powerful tool for adding complexity and interest to a composition, and it can be effectively employed in guitar music.

UNDERSTANDING METRIC MODULATION

In metric modulation, a new rhythmic value is introduced, and the tempo is adjusted accordingly. This can involve changing from one time signature to another or shifting the emphasis within the existing time signature.

The relationship between the old and new rhythms is often expressed as a ratio. For example, a quarter note in the old rhythm may become an eighth note in the new rhythm.

Experimenting with Metric Modulation in Guitar Composition:

Identify the Old and New Rhythms: Determine the current rhythm (old rhythm) and the desired new rhythm. This could involve changing from quarter notes to eighth notes or shifting from a simple meter to a compound meter.

Establish the Old Rhythm Clearly:

Before introducing the new rhythm, establish the old rhythm clearly so that listeners are aware of the existing pulse.

Introduce the New Rhythm Gradually:

Transition into the new rhythm smoothly. This can be done by gradually emphasizing the new rhythmic value until it becomes the perceived pulse.

Example 1: Transitioning from 4/4 to 6/8:

```
| Old Rhythm (4/4)        | New Rhythm (6/8)        |
|-------------------------|-------------------------|
| 1  2  3  4  1  2  3 | 1  2  3  4  5  6  |
| D  UD  UD  UD  U |D  UD  UD  U       |
```

In this example, the old rhythm is a simple 4/4 pattern with down-up strumming. The new rhythm introduces a 6/8 feel with a triplet strumming pattern. The transition gradually shifts the emphasis to the eighth note triplets, creating a metric modulation.

Example 2: Changing from 4/4 to 5/4:

```
| Old Rhythm (4/4)      | New Rhythm (5/4)        |
|----------------------|-------------------------|
| 1  2  3  4  1  2  3 | 1  2  3  4  5      |
| D  UD  UD  UD  U | D  UD  UD  U      |
```

Here, the old rhythm is a typical 4/4 strumming pattern. The new rhythm introduces a 5/4 time signature, creating a shift in the perceived pulse.

Experimentation and Variation:

Change of Subdivision: Experiment with changing the subdivision within the same time signature. For example, transition from eighth notes to triplet eighth notes.

Dynamic Changes: Use metric modulation to accompany dynamic changes in your composition. For instance, shift from a slow, spacious rhythm to a more rapid and intricate feel.

Incorporate Guitar Techniques: Utilize various guitar techniques like hammer-ons, pull-offs, or slides to enhance the effect of the metric modulation.

Gradual Transitions:

Smooth Blending: Gradually blend the old and new rhythms to avoid abrupt shifts. This can involve overlapping patterns or using transitional phrases that incorporate elements of both rhythms.

Listening and Adjusting:

Listen Critically: Regularly listen to your composition to ensure that the metric modulation enhances the overall flow without disrupting the musical continuity.

Adjust as Needed: Make adjustments to the transition points or the emphasis of the new rhythmic values based on how it feels within the context of your composition.

Collaboration with Drummer or Band:

Coordinate with Other Instruments: If you are working with a drummer or other instrumentalists, coordinate the metric modulation to ensure a unified and synchronized performance.

By experimenting with metric modulation in your guitar compositions, you can introduce intriguing rhythmic changes that captivate listeners and elevate the complexity of your music. It's a powerful tool for expressing creativity and pushing the boundaries of traditional rhythmic structures.

RHYTHMIC TENSION

Use changing time signatures to build rhythmic tension leading up to a climax or significant moment in your composition. The shifting meter can heighten anticipation.

BUILD RHYTHMIC TENSION WITH CHANGING SIGNATURES

Building rhythmic tension through changing time signatures in guitar composition can add a layer of complexity and excitement to your music. Changing time signatures creates an element of surprise and challenge for both the performer and the listener.

Understanding Changing Time Signatures:

Time signatures dictate the number of beats in a measure and the type of note that receives the beat. Changing time signatures involves transitioning between different rhythmic frameworks, which can include alterations in the number of beats per measure or the subdivision of beats.

Plan the Structure:

Map Out Sections: Identify the sections of your composition where changing time signatures can enhance the rhythmic tension. Common points for signature changes include transitions between verses and choruses or leading into a climactic section.

Consider Musical Phrases: Align time signature changes with the natural phrasing of your melody or lyrics. This ensures that the shifts feel organic and purposeful.

Gradual Progression:

Start Simple: Begin with a stable time signature before introducing changes. This establishes a foundation and allows listeners to establish a rhythmic expectation.

Gradual Complexity: Introduce changes gradually. For example, move from a common time signature (4/4) to an odd meter (e.g., 7/8) in a progressive manner to build tension.

Create Contrast:

Use Odd Meters: Experiment with odd meters like 5/4, 7/8, or 9/8 to create rhythmic tension. The uneven grouping of beats adds an unpredictable and dynamic feel to your composition.

Contrast with Simple Meters: After using an odd meter, contrast it with a return to a more straightforward time signature (e.g., 4/4). This can create a sense of resolution or a release of tension.

Syncopation and Offbeat Accents:

Syncopated Patterns: Incorporate syncopated rhythms and offbeat accents within the changing time signatures. This adds a layer of complexity and can heighten the rhythmic tension.

Emphasize Weak Beats: Highlight weak beats in the measure to create a sense of instability. This can be achieved through accents or dynamic playing on offbeats.

Experiment with Polyrhythms:

Overlay Different Rhythmic Patterns: Experiment with polyrhythms, where different rhythmic patterns coexist simultaneously. This can be achieved by playing one rhythm with your melody and another with accompanying chords.

Layered Phrasing: Layer different time signatures in different instrumental parts. For example, have the guitar playing in 5/4 while the drums maintain a 4/4 pattern, creating rhythmic tension through the contrast.

Dynamic Changes:

Couple with Dynamic Shifts: Coordinate time signature changes with dynamic shifts in your composition. For instance, a transition to an odd meter can be accompanied by an increase in intensity or volume.

Transitional Phrases:

Smooth Transitions: Design transitional phrases that lead into the new time signature. This helps the listener adjust to the change and makes the transition feel intentional.

Use Repeated Motifs: Repeat rhythmic motifs across different time signatures to create a sense of continuity while still introducing tension.

Collaboration with Other Instruments:

Coordinate with Drummer and Bassist: If you're working with other musicians, especially a drummer and bassist, collaborate on the transitions and make sure everyone is synchronized during the signature changes.

Listen Critically and Adjust:

Regularly Review and Adjust: Listen to your composition critically and adjust the time signature changes as needed. Make sure they serve the overall musical narrative and don't feel forced.

By strategically incorporating changing time signatures into your guitar compositions, you can create rhythmic tension that captivates your audience and adds a unique dimension to your musical expression. Experiment with these techniques, and find the balance that works best for your creative vision.

TIME SIGNATURE AND EMOTION

Consider the emotional impact of different time signatures. A 6/8 meter may convey a flowing and relaxed feel, while 7/8 can introduce a sense of urgency or unpredictability.

USING TIME SIGNATURES TO CONVEY EMOTION

Time signatures play a crucial role in shaping the rhythmic foundation of a musical composition, and they can be used to convey a wide range of emotions in guitar music. By choosing specific time signatures and rhythmic patterns, you can evoke different moods and intensify the emotional impact of your composition.

Selecting Time Signatures:

Common Time (4/4): Often associated with stability and a sense of normalcy, 4/4 time signature is widely used in various genres. It can convey emotions ranging from comfort to neutrality.

3/4 and 6/8: These time signatures, associated with waltzes and triple meter, can create a sense of flowing elegance or even nostalgia. They are often used to convey more emotive and contemplative moods.

Odd Meters (e.g., 5/4, 7/8): Odd time signatures can introduce tension and unpredictability, making them suitable for conveying a sense of urgency, unrest, or complexity.

Adjusting Tempo:

Slow Tempos: Slow tempos in any time signature can convey emotions like melancholy, introspection, or relaxation. A slower pace allows for more deliberate and emotive expression on the guitar.

Fast Tempos: Faster tempos, especially in odd meters, can create a sense of excitement, urgency, or even anxiety. They are well-suited for conveying energetic or intense emotions.

Dynamic Changes:

Dynamic Contrast: Utilize dynamic changes within a time signature to convey emotion. Gradual swells and fades, along with changes in picking intensity, can evoke feelings of tension, release, or passion.

Syncopation and Accentuation:

Syncopated Rhythms: Introduce syncopation to create unexpected accents or offbeat patterns. Syncopation can add a sense of surprise and can be used to convey emotions such as playfulness, excitement, or unease.

Accentuation: Use accents on certain beats or notes to highlight specific emotions. Strong accents can convey power or urgency, while subtle accents can evoke a more delicate or nuanced emotion.

Polyrhythms and Complex Patterns:

Polyrhythmic Elements: Incorporate polyrhythmic elements where different rhythmic patterns coexist. This complexity can convey a sense of sophistication, tension, or intricate emotion.

Changing Subdivisions: Experiment with changing subdivisions within a time signature. Shifting between straight and triplet feels, for example, can evoke different emotions and add variety to your composition.

Use of Rubato:

Rubato (Expressive Timing): Introduce rubato, a technique where the tempo is temporarily sped up or slowed down for expressive purposes. This can be employed to convey a sense of freedom, emotion, or introspection.

Harmonic Choices:

Harmonic Progressions: Combine time signatures with specific harmonic progressions to enhance emotional expression. For example, unresolved or dissonant chords in an odd meter can create a feeling of tension or anticipation.

Consider the Context:

Contextual Awareness: Be aware of the overall context of your composition and the emotions you want to convey in specific sections. The interaction of harmonic, melodic, and rhythmic elements contributes to the overall emotional impact.

Experimentation:

Trial and Error: Experiment with different time signatures and rhythmic patterns. Sometimes, unexpected combinations can lead to unique emotional expressions.

Reflect Personal Feelings:

Personal Expression: Let your own emotions and feelings guide your choices. Music is a powerful form of personal expression, and your connection to the composition will resonate with your audience.

Example:

Consider a piece in 6/8 time with a slow tempo and a gentle picking pattern. The flowing nature of 6/8, combined with the deliberate pacing, can convey a sense of introspection, nostalgia, or even sadness. The choice of chords and the addition of legato phrasing can further enhance these emotions.

On the other hand, a composition in 7/8 with a fast-paced strumming pattern and syncopated accents might convey a sense of urgency, excitement, or complexity. The odd meter adds an element of unpredictability, and the faster tempo intensifies the emotional impact.

In conclusion, time signatures are a powerful tool for shaping the emotional landscape of your guitar compositions. By thoughtfully selecting time signatures, adjusting tempo, incorporating rhythmic elements, and experimenting with different approaches, you can create music that resonates with a wide range of emotions and connects with your audience on a deep level.

SIGNATURE RHYTHMIC PATTERNS

Develop signature rhythmic patterns associated with specific time signatures. These patterns can become motifs that define the rhythmic identity of your composition.

CREATE SIGNATURE RHYTHMIC PATTERNS

Developing signature rhythmic patterns associated with specific time signatures in guitar composition involves creating distinctive and recognizable rhythmic motifs that suit the mood and feel of a particular time signature. These patterns contribute to the overall character of the composition and help define its rhythmic identity.

Understand the Time Signature:

Analyze the Meter: Understand the natural accents and emphasis of the time signature. Identify strong beats, weak beats, and any unusual subdivisions that define the meter.

Explore Basic Patterns:

Start Simple: Begin by experimenting with basic rhythmic patterns that align with the time signature. Use standard strumming or picking patterns to establish a foundation.

Experiment with Subdivisions:

Vary Subdivisions: Explore different subdivisions within the time signature. For example, experiment with eighth notes, triplets, or sixteenth notes to create variation and interest.

Accentuation and Dynamics:

Accent Strong Beats: Emphasize the strong beats of the time signature to provide clarity and definition. This can be achieved through dynamic picking or strumming.

Dynamic Variations: Introduce dynamic variations within the pattern. Play some notes louder than others to create a sense of movement and contour.

Syncopation and Offbeat Accents:

Syncopated Patterns: Incorporate syncopation by placing accents on offbeats or weak beats. This adds complexity and a sense of groove to the rhythmic pattern.

Offbeat Accents: Experiment with emphasizing offbeat notes or creating patterns where the accents fall between the standard beats.

Create Repeating Motifs:

Develop Motifs: Design short rhythmic motifs that can be repeated throughout the composition. These motifs serve as signature patterns and contribute to the overall coherence of the piece.

Variations on a Theme: Experiment with variations of the initial motif to keep the rhythmic pattern interesting and evolving.

Explore Polyrhythms:

Layer Different Rhythms: Introduce polyrhythmic elements by layering different rhythmic patterns. This can involve playing two or more contrasting patterns simultaneously.

Cross-Rhythms: Experiment with cross-rhythms, where one rhythmic pattern in a different subdivision overlaps with the main pattern. This adds complexity and depth.

Consider Harmonic Progressions:

Align with Chord Changes: Coordinate your rhythmic patterns with harmonic progressions. Adjust the rhythmic intensity based on the emotional or harmonic context.

Example 1: 4/4 Time Signature – Straight Rock Pattern:

```plaintext
| 1  2  3  4 | 1  2  3  4 |
| D  UD UD  | D  UD UD  |
```

This is a classic straight rock pattern in 4/4 time. The down-up strumming motion aligns with the straightforward feel of the meter.

Example 2: 6/8 Time Signature – Waltz Pattern:

```plaintext
| 1  2  3  4  5  6  | 1  2  3  4  5  6  |
| D  D  UD  UD  U  | D  D  UD  UD  U  |
```

This is a waltz pattern in 6/8 time. The emphasis on the first beat and the use of triplets create a flowing and elegant feel.

Example 3: 7/8 Time Signature – Odd Meter Pattern:

```

| 1  2  3  4  5  6  7  | 1  2  3  4  5  6  7  |
| D  UD  UD  D  UD  U  | D  UD  UD  D  UD  U  |
```

This is a pattern in 7/8 time with a syncopated feel. The odd meter introduces an element of tension and unpredictability.

Experiment and Adapt:

Trial and Error: Be open to experimentation. Try different rhythmic patterns and see how they fit with the overall composition.

Adapt to the Composition: The signature rhythmic patterns should serve the emotional and structural needs of your composition. Make adjustments based on the context of the music.

Listen Critically:

Evaluate the Sound: Regularly listen to how your rhythmic patterns contribute to the overall sound of the composition. Make refinements as needed to achieve the desired emotional impact.

By developing signature rhythmic patterns associated with specific time signatures, you add a unique and recognizable touch to your guitar compositions. These patterns become an integral part of the composition's identity, contributing to the emotional depth and musical cohesion.

TIME SIGNATURE CHANGE AND SONG STRUCTURE

Integrate changes in time signatures into the overall structure of your composition. Use them strategically to mark the beginning or end of sections.

INTEGRATING TIME SIGNATURE CHANGES WITH SONG STRUCTURE

Integrating changes in time signatures into the overall structure of your guitar composition requires thoughtful planning and execution to ensure a seamless and musically engaging transition. Time signature changes can add complexity, interest, and unique rhythmic flavors to your music.

Establish a Clear Foundation:

Start with a Stable Time Signature: Begin your composition with a stable and commonly used time signature to establish a foundation. This helps listeners develop a rhythmic reference point.

Identify Musical Sections for Change:

Analyze the Musical Phrasing: Identify natural breaks, transitions, or sections where a change in time signature would enhance the musical narrative. Consider shifts between verses, choruses, or instrumental breaks.

Match Changes to Mood: Align time signature changes with the emotional or dynamic shifts in your composition. A change in time signature can accentuate changes in mood or intensity.

Plan Smooth Transitions:

Gradual vs. Abrupt Transitions: Decide whether you want the time signature change to be gradual or abrupt. Gradual transitions involve changing subdivisions or gradually shifting emphasis, while abrupt changes create a more noticeable contrast.

Use Transitional Phrases: Design transitional phrases that lead into the new time signature. These phrases can bridge the gap between the old and new rhythms, making the change feel intentional.

Consideration for the Listener:

Maintain Listener Engagement: Keep the listener engaged by introducing changes at points where their attention is naturally focused. Avoid introducing complex changes during highly intricate or attention-demanding sections.

Experiment with Polymeters:

Explore Polymetric Sections: Experiment with polymeters, where different instruments or parts play in different time signatures simultaneously. This can create an intricate layering effect.

Use a Common Pulse: Ensure that there is a shared pulse or beat that ties together the different time signatures, preventing the composition from feeling disjointed.

Align with Melodic and Harmonic Elements:

Coordinate with Chord Changes: If your composition involves chord changes, coordinate time signature changes with these shifts to maintain harmonic cohesion.

Match Melodic Phrasing: Align the timing of time signature changes with the natural phrasing of your melody. This creates a more organic and integrated feel.

Practice and Refinement:

Rehearse Transitions: Practice the transitions between different time signatures to ensure that they feel smooth and are executed with precision.

Refine Based on Feel: Listen to how the changes feel within the context of your composition. Make adjustments to timing, dynamics, or phrasing as needed.

Consider Collaboration:

Collaborate with Other Musicians: If you are working with other musicians, particularly a drummer or bassist, collaborate on the timing and execution of time signature changes. Consistent communication is essential.

Example 1: Transition from 4/4 to 7/8:

```
| 1  2  3  4  | 1  2  3  4  5  6  7  |
| D  U D  U D  | D  U D  D  U D  U    |
```

In this example, a gradual transition from a standard 4/4 time signature to 7/8 occurs by emphasizing the 7/8 subdivision while maintaining the original strumming pattern.

Example 2: Abrupt Shift from 3/4 to 5/4:

```
|1  2  3  |1  2  3  4  5  |
|D  UD  |D  UD  D  U    |
```

In this example, an abrupt shift from 3/4 to 5/4 occurs with a change in the strumming pattern, creating a noticeable and intentional contrast.

Listen to Feedback:

Seek Feedback: Share your composition with others and seek feedback on how the time signature changes are perceived. Adjustments based on listener feedback can enhance the overall effectiveness.

Maintain Consistency in Structure:

Overall Cohesiveness: Ensure that the changes in time signatures contribute to the overall cohesiveness of your composition. Aim for a balanced structure that enhances rather than disrupts the flow.

Serve the Musical Narrative:

Align with the Narrative: Keep in mind that time signature changes should serve the musical narrative and emotional expression of your composition. Ensure that they enhance the overall impact of the music.

Integrating changes in time signatures is a powerful way to add depth and interest to your guitar compositions. Thoughtful planning, smooth transitions, and a consideration of the musical context will contribute to a more compelling and engaging musical experience for both you and your audience.

FREE TIME

Explore sections with free time, where the music temporarily breaks away from a strict meter. Free time allows for expressive, rubato-like playing.

EXPERIMENTING WITH FREE TIME

Experimenting with free time, also known as rubato or tempo rubato, in guitar composition provides a unique opportunity for rhythmic development and expressive freedom. Free time allows for a more flexible approach to rhythm, allowing the guitarist to stretch or compress certain phrases for emotional impact.

Understand Rubato:

Definition: Rubato is a term that indicates a flexible, expressive manipulation of tempo. It allows for rhythmic freedom, with certain notes or phrases being played faster or slower than the established tempo.

Identify Appropriate Sections:

Select Emotional or Expressive Phrases: Choose sections of your composition that carry emotional weight or require heightened expression. This could include solos, climactic moments, or lyrical passages.

Avoid Excessive Use: While rubato offers expressive freedom, be mindful not to use it excessively. Selective application enhances musical expression, while too much can lead to a loss of rhythmic cohesion.

Experiment with Tempo Fluctuations:

Gradual Tempo Changes: Experiment with gradually slowing down or speeding up the tempo within a phrase or section. This can create a sense of tension and release.

Jerky Changes: Introduce sudden tempo changes for dramatic effect. Abrupt shifts in tempo can evoke surprise or intensity.

Explore Dynamic Contrasts:

Connect Dynamics with Tempo: Coordinate dynamic changes with tempo fluctuations. For instance, soften the volume during slower sections and increase it during faster passages.

Vary Articulation: Experiment with different articulations such as legato, staccato, or hammer-ons/pull-offs to complement the rubato phrasing.

Use Rubato in Chord Progressions:

Stretching Chord Changes: Apply rubato to chord progressions by stretching or compressing the time between chord changes. This adds a flowing, expressive quality to the harmonic structure.

Breaking Rigid Rhythms: Free time can be particularly effective when breaking away from rigid rhythmic patterns, allowing for more nuanced and emotive playing.

Experiment with Melodic Lines:

Expressive Melodies: Apply rubato to melodic lines, especially in instances where you want to emphasize the emotional content of the melody.

Microtiming: Experiment with microtiming within a phrase, subtly delaying or advancing certain notes for added expressiveness.

Collaborate with Other Instruments:

Coordinate with Other Musicians: If you are working with other musicians, communicate your intentions regarding rubato. Collaborate to ensure that the tempo changes are synchronized for a unified performance.

Record and Listen:

Record Your Playing: Record your experimentation with rubato to listen critically to the nuances of your performance.

Evaluate Effectiveness: Assess how well the rubato enhances the emotional impact and overall flow of the composition.

Explore Different Genres:

Adapt to Genre Characteristics: Consider the characteristics of the genre you're working in. Rubato is versatile and can be applied in various styles, from classical to jazz to folk.

Fusion of Styles: Experiment with combining rubato sections with more structured, rhythmic elements for a fusion of styles within your composition.

Maintain a Sense of Pulse:

Retain Internal Pulse: Even in free time, maintain a sense of internal pulse. This ensures that the rubato sections still feel connected to the overall rhythmic structure.

Use Metronome as a Reference: Experiment with a metronome as a reference during rubato sections, especially when rehearsing or recording with other musicians.

Consider Silence and Pauses:

Strategic Pauses: Introduce strategic pauses within rubato sections. Silence can be a powerful expressive tool and adds to the overall dynamic range.

Example:

Consider a lyrical guitar solo in a ballad where rubato is employed to emphasize certain poignant phrases. The guitarist may slow down slightly before reaching a climactic note and then speed up during the resolution. This intentional manipulation of tempo enhances the emotional impact of the solo.

Experimenting with free time in guitar composition provides an avenue for personal expression and emotional depth. The key is to use rubato judiciously, enhancing the overall musical narrative without sacrificing rhythmic coherence. As you explore the possibilities of free time, you'll discover new ways to infuse your compositions with expressive nuance and captivate your audience.

TIME SIGNATURE CHANGES AND MELODIC PHRASING

Coordinate changes in time signatures with melodic phrasing. Consider transitioning between meters at points where it enhances the natural flow of the melody.

COORDINATING TIME SIGNATURE CHANGES WITH MELODIC PHRASING

Coordinating time signature changes with melodic phrasing in guitar composition is a sophisticated approach that can enhance rhythmic development, add complexity to your music, and create a seamless fusion between melody and rhythm.

Understand the Relationship:

Analyzing Melodic Phrasing: Break down your melody into distinct phrases. Identify points where the melodic contour suggests rhythmic variations or where a change in time signature could enhance the emotional impact.

Match Time Signatures to Phrases: Select time signatures that complement the natural rhythm and pacing of your melodic phrases.

Establish a Clear Melodic Structure:

Define Melodic Sections: Clearly define different sections of your melody. This could include verses, choruses, or distinct themes within the composition.

Identify Climaxes or Resolution Points: Pinpoint moments within the melody that act as climaxes, resolutions, or points of tension. These moments are prime candidates for time signature changes.

Gradual Transitions:

Smooth Tempo Changes: Use gradual transitions between time signatures to avoid abrupt shifts. Gradual changes provide a smoother and more organic flow.

Utilize Transitional Phrases: Craft transitional phrases that lead from one time signature to another. These phrases help the listener adjust to the changing rhythmic structure.

Align Time Signatures with Phrasing:

Emphasize Key Moments: Align changes in time signature with key moments in your melodic phrasing. For example, introduce a time signature change at the beginning of a powerful guitar riff or an emotive lyrical line.

Accentuate Melodic Contours: Use time signature changes to accentuate the rising and falling contours of your melody. This adds dynamic interest to the overall composition.

Incorporate Odd Meters for Expressiveness:

Use Odd Meters Thoughtfully: Experiment with odd meters (e.g., 5/4, 7/8) to add expressiveness and complexity. Odd meters can create a sense of unpredictability and intrigue when aligned with specific melodic phrases.

Match Odd Meters to Melodic Phrasing: Choose odd meters that naturally fit the rhythmic structure of your melodic phrases. This ensures that the time signature changes enhance rather than disrupt the melodic flow.

Dynamic Changes in Melody:

Coordinate with Dynamic Shifts: Align time signature changes with dynamic shifts in your melody. For instance, introduce a time signature change as the melody builds towards a crescendo.

Enhance Emotional Content: Use time signature changes to enhance the emotional content of your melody, creating a stronger connection with the listener.

Experiment with Polyrhythms:

Layer Rhythmic Patterns: Experiment with polyrhythmic elements, where different rhythmic patterns coexist. This can involve playing one rhythm with your melody and another with accompanying chords.

Maintain Clarity: While experimenting with polyrhythms, ensure that the complexity doesn't overshadow the clarity of the melody. The goal is to enhance, not overwhelm.

Coordinate with Chord Changes:

Harmonic Alignment: Align time signature changes with chord changes. This creates a harmonically and rhythmically integrated composition.

Create Tension and Release: Introduce time signature changes during moments of harmonic tension or resolution, adding a layer of rhythmic tension and release.

Record and Evaluate:

Recording is Key: Record your composition to evaluate how well the time signature changes align with your melodic phrasing.

Adjust as Needed: Listen critically and make adjustments to the timing of the time signature changes to achieve the desired rhythmic and melodic synergy.

Collaborate with Other Instruments:

Communicate with Other Musicians: If working with other musicians, communicate the planned time signature changes. Ensure that all instruments are synchronized to maintain a cohesive musical performance.

Consider the Genre's Characteristics:

Adapt to Genre Elements: Consider the characteristics of the musical genre you're working in. Some genres may naturally lend themselves to more fluid time signature changes, while others may require subtler shifts.

Example:

Consider a guitar composition with a melodic phrase building up to a climactic point. As the melody reaches its peak, you introduce a change from 4/4 to 6/8 to elongate certain notes and add an expressive twist. This shift enhances the emotional intensity of the melody before resolving back to 4/4 as the phrase concludes.

Coordinating time signature changes with melodic phrasing is a powerful tool for enhancing rhythmic development in your guitar compositions. Thoughtful planning, experimentation, and a keen ear for how these elements interact will contribute to a rich and dynamic musical experience for both you as the guitarist and your audience.

CULTURAL INFLUENCES

Explore time signatures associated with different cultural influences. For example, certain time signatures are prevalent in specific world music traditions, adding a cross-cultural dimension to your composition.

EXPLORE CULTURAL INFLUENCES

Exploring time signatures associated with different cultural influences in guitar composition can add a rich and diverse dimension to your music. Different cultures have distinct rhythmic patterns that are often reflected in their traditional music. Incorporating these time signatures into your guitar compositions allows you to infuse your music with the flavors of various cultural traditions.

Research Cultural Rhythms:

Study Traditional Music: Research the traditional music of various cultures. Explore how different regions and societies interpret rhythm and time signatures in their music.

Understand Percussion Instruments: Many cultures express their rhythmic identity through percussion instruments. Understand the unique rhythms played on instruments like drums, hand percussion, or traditional stringed instruments.

Learn Time Signatures:

Identify Traditional Time Signatures: Learn about the time signatures commonly used in traditional music of different cultures. Time signatures may include both common meters (4/4, 3/4) and more exotic ones (e.g., 7/8, 5/4).

Associations with Dance: Some time signatures are closely associated with specific dance forms in certain cultures. Understanding these connections can provide insight into the rhythmic feel.

EXAMPLES OF CULTURAL TIME SIGNATURES

West African (e.g., Mali):

Time Signatures: 12/8, 6/8, 4/4 with intricate polyrhythms.

Influence on Guitar Composition: Incorporate polyrhythmic patterns, layered rhythms, and syncopation into your guitar compositions.

Flamenco (Spain):

Time Signatures: Commonly 12/8, 3/4, and variations of 4/4.

Influence on Guitar Composition: Use rasgueado techniques, emphasize rhythmic accents, and experiment with the Phrygian mode for an authentic flamenco feel.

Indian Classical (e.g., Raga music):

Time Signatures: Jhaptaal (10 beats), Ektaal (12 beats), Tintal (16 beats).

Influence on Guitar Composition: Experiment with the intricate rhythms of Indian classical music, explore sitar-like melodic patterns, and use slides and bends for expressive phrasing.

Irish Folk Music:

Time Signatures: Commonly in 6/8, 9/8, and occasionally 12/8.

Influence on Guitar Composition: Incorporate fingerpicking techniques, use open tunings, and experiment with jigs and reels to capture the essence of Irish folk rhythms.

Balkan Music (e.g., Bulgaria):

Time Signatures: 7/8, 9/8, 11/8, and asymmetrical meters.

Influence on Guitar Composition: Explore complex rhythms, odd meters, and incorporate rapid picking techniques for a Balkan folk feel.

Japanese Traditional Music:

Time Signatures: Varied, including 2/4, 4/4, and 7/8.

Influence on Guitar Composition: Embrace simplicity, use pentatonic scales, and experiment with plucked string techniques to capture the elegance of Japanese traditional music.

Blend Cultural Influences:

Create Fusion: Experiment with blending elements from different cultural influences within a single composition. This can result in a unique and eclectic sound that reflects your diverse musical influences.

Respectful Integration: Approach the integration of cultural elements with respect and sensitivity. Aim to celebrate the diversity of musical traditions rather than appropriating them.

Experiment with Hybrid Styles:

Combine Genres: Explore hybrid styles that merge traditional rhythms from different cultures with contemporary guitar techniques. For example, fuse West African rhythms with rock guitar riffs.

Incorporate World Music Instruments: Experiment with incorporating instruments traditionally associated with certain cultures, such as the djembe for African rhythms or the tabla for Indian influences.

Explore Folklore and Storytelling:

Tell Stories Through Music: Use your guitar compositions to tell stories inspired by cultural folklore. Let the rhythms and time signatures convey the emotions and narratives associated with different cultural tales.

Immerse Yourself in Recordings:

Listen Actively: Immerse yourself in recordings of traditional music from various cultures. Pay attention to the nuances of rhythm, time signatures, and instrumentation.

Adapt Ideas: Take inspiration from traditional compositions and adapt rhythmic ideas into your guitar work.

Collaborate with Musicians from Different Backgrounds:

Expand Horizons: Collaborate with musicians from diverse cultural backgrounds. Their insights and contributions can enrich your understanding of different rhythmic traditions.

Learn From Others: Engage in musical dialogue, learn from their rhythmic vocabulary, and incorporate elements from their cultural background into your compositions.

Attend Cultural Events:

Live Performances: Attend live performances of traditional music from different cultures. Experience the rhythms firsthand and observe how musicians express themselves within their cultural context.

Workshops and Seminars: Participate in workshops or seminars conducted by musicians proficient in traditional styles. Gain hands-on experience and ask questions to deepen your understanding.

Exploring time signatures associated with different cultural influences in guitar composition allows you to celebrate the diversity of musical traditions and create compositions that resonate with a global audience. By studying, respecting, and integrating elements from various cultures, you can enrich your musical palette and contribute to the cross-cultural dialogue through your guitar compositions.

SHAPING DYNAMICS

Use changes in time signatures to shape the dynamics of your composition. A shift to an odd meter can introduce intensity, while a return to a common time signature may provide resolution.

USING TIME SIGNATURES TO SHAPE DYNAMICS

Using changes in time signatures to shape the dynamics of a guitar composition can be a powerful technique to add variety, interest, and emotional depth to your music. Time signature changes impact the rhythmic structure, influencing the way listeners perceive the flow and intensity of the composition.

Define Sections and Phrases:

Identify Musical Phrases: Break down your composition into distinct musical phrases or sections. This could include verses, choruses, bridges, or instrumental solos.

Recognize Dynamics: Assess the inherent dynamics within each section. Note where you want to create contrast, build tension, or introduce a sense of release.

Choose Appropriate Time Signatures:

Match Time Signatures to Emotion: Select time signatures that align with the emotional content and energy you want to convey in each section. For example, a shift from a common time signature like 4/4 to an odd meter like 7/8 can introduce tension and excitement.

Vary Time Signatures: Experiment with a variety of time signatures to create dynamic contrast. This could involve alternating between simple and compound meters or using asymmetrical time signatures for a more complex feel.

Experiment with Tempo Changes:

Adjust Tempo Accordingly: Consider adjusting the tempo along with the time signature changes. A faster tempo in a section with an odd time signature may heighten the sense of urgency, while a slower tempo in a common time signature might evoke a more relaxed mood.

Gradual Tempo Shifts: Experiment with gradual tempo shifts to smoothly transition between sections. Gradual accelerandos or ritardandos can enhance the fluidity of the changes.

Highlight Structural Elements:

Use Time Signature Changes as Landmarks: Make time signature changes coincide with important structural elements like the beginning of a chorus, the climax of a solo, or the resolution of a musical tension. This draws attention to these critical points in the composition.

Emphasize Transitions: If your composition has distinct transitions between sections, consider placing time signature changes at these points to emphasize the shift in mood or intensity.

Create Tension and Release:

Leverage Odd Time Signatures: Introduce odd time signatures to create tension and unpredictability. The irregular grouping of beats can make listeners feel a sense of anticipation and excitement.

Resolution in Common Time: Resolve tension by returning to a common time signature. This can provide a sense of stability and resolution, especially after a section with an odd meter.

Syncopation and Accentuation:

Explore Syncopated Rhythms: Introduce syncopation during sections with time signature changes. This adds complexity and can contribute to the dynamic feel of the composition.

Accentuate Key Beats: Experiment with accentuating certain beats within the new time signature. Strong accents can heighten the impact of the change.

Consider Harmonic Progressions:

Coordinate with Chord Changes: Align time signature changes with key harmonic progressions. The rhythmic shifts can complement the harmonic movements, enhancing the overall impact.

Match Rhythm to Harmony: Adjust your rhythmic patterns to align with the emotional content of the accompanying chords. This coordination reinforces the dynamic expression of the composition.

Use Rubato and Expressive Timing:

Introduce Rubato: During transitions or in sections with time signature changes, incorporate rubato. This expressive timing technique allows for a flexible tempo and adds a personal touch to your playing.

Expressive Phrasing: Use expressive phrasing, such as slowing down or speeding up certain melodic lines, to complement the changing rhythms. This contributes to the overall dynamic shaping of the composition.

Experiment with Polyrhythms:

Layer Different Rhythmic Patterns: Experiment with polyrhythmic elements, where different rhythmic patterns coexist. This complexity adds depth to the composition and can influence the perceived dynamics.

Coordinate Polyrhythms: Ensure that polyrhythmic elements are coordinated and contribute to the overall dynamic expression. Polyrhythms can be a powerful tool when used intentionally.

Example:

Consider a composition that starts in 4/4 with a moderate tempo for the verses, creating a stable and familiar foundation. As the chorus approaches, transition to 5/4 with a faster tempo, introducing a sense of urgency and excitement. The odd meter creates tension, and when resolving back to 4/4 for the next verse, there's a release of that tension.

Using changes in time signatures strategically allows you to shape the dynamics of your guitar composition, guiding the listener through a dynamic and engaging musical journey. Whether it's creating tension, emphasizing key structural elements, or introducing unexpected twists, the artful incorporation of time signature changes enhances the expressiveness and impact of your music.

TEMPO AND SIGNATURE CHANGES

Coordinate changes in time signatures with tempo adjustments. Tempo changes can further enhance the impact of shifting meters.

CONSIDER TEMPO CHANGES WITH SIGNATURE CHANGES

Coordinating changes in time signatures with tempo adjustments in guitar composition is a sophisticated technique that can bring depth, complexity, and dynamic interest to your music. The interplay between time signatures and tempo changes allows you to shape the rhythmic structure in a nuanced way.

Understand the Relationship:

Recognize Time-Tempo Interaction: Understand the intrinsic relationship between time signatures and tempo. Changes in time signatures can influence the perceived pace of your music.

Adjusting Tempo for Flow: Use tempo adjustments to ensure a smooth transition between different time signatures, maintaining a coherent and flowing musical experience.

Select Key Sections for Changes:

Identify Musical Phrases: Choose specific musical phrases, sections, or transitions where changes in time signatures will enhance the overall dynamic and rhythmic character of your composition.

Align with Emotional Content: Consider aligning time signature changes with sections that carry emotional weight or require a heightened level of energy.

Gradual Transitions:

Smooth Tempo Shifts: When changing time signatures, experiment with gradual tempo transitions to maintain musical fluidity. Gradual shifts provide a more natural and organic feel.

Use Transitional Phrases: Craft transitional phrases that guide the listener smoothly from one time signature to another. This helps avoid abrupt disruptions in the musical flow.

Emphasize Specific Beats:

Align Tempo Changes with Accentuation: Coordinate tempo adjustments with accents within the new time signature. Emphasizing specific beats enhances the effectiveness of both the time signature change and the tempo shift.

Explore Syncopation: Experiment with syncopated rhythms during transitions to create anticipation and excitement. This can be achieved by accenting offbeats or introducing unexpected rhythmic patterns.

Experiment with Tempo Mapping:

Create Tempo Maps: Develop a tempo map for your composition that outlines where changes in time signatures occur and how they correspond to shifts in tempo.

Consider Metronome Markings: Assign specific metronome markings to each section, ensuring that the tempo adjustments align with the rhythmic character you intend to convey.

Highlight Climaxes and Transitions:

Tempo as a Dramatic Tool: Use tempo changes to emphasize climactic moments, transitions between sections, or shifts in intensity. This enhances the dramatic impact of your composition.

Acceleration for Climaxes: Consider accelerating the tempo as you approach climactic sections, creating a sense of urgency and building tension.

Experiment with Odd Meters:

Dynamic Shifts with Odd Meters: Introduce odd meters with corresponding tempo adjustments for dynamic shifts. Odd meters can create a unique rhythmic intensity that is enhanced by tempo changes.

Odd Meter Example: Transitioning from 4/4 to 7/8 can involve a subtle acceleration to maintain the energy and intensity in the composition.

Consider Genre Characteristics:

Adapt to Genre Styles: Consider the characteristics of the genre you are working in. Some genres may naturally accommodate frequent tempo changes, while others benefit from subtler adjustments.

Blend Fusion Styles: In fusion genres, blending elements from different musical styles may involve more frequent and pronounced tempo adjustments.

Record and Evaluate:

Critical Listening: Record your composition and actively listen to how the changes in time signatures align with tempo adjustments.

Adjust as Needed: Evaluate the effectiveness of the coordination and make adjustments to the timing of tempo changes to achieve the desired rhythmic and dynamic balance.

Collaborate with Other Musicians:

Coordinate with Ensemble: If collaborating with other musicians, communicate the planned changes in time signatures and tempo adjustments. Ensure that all instruments are synchronized for a cohesive performance.

Rehearse Together: Practice transitions with the ensemble to ensure that tempo adjustments are well-coordinated and enhance the overall musical expression.

Example:

Consider a guitar composition that starts with a moderate 4/4 time signature in the verse. As it transitions to the chorus with a 7/8 time signature, the tempo subtly accelerates to maintain energy and drive. Returning to the verse in 4/4 involves a gradual deceleration to restore a more relaxed pace.

Coordinating changes in time signatures with tempo adjustments in your guitar composition provides a sophisticated means of shaping the dynamic and rhythmic character of your music. Thoughtful planning, experimentation, and a keen ear for how time and tempo interact will contribute to a more engaging and expressive musical experience for both you as the guitarist and your audience.

MINIMALISM

Explore minimalist approaches, where a repetitive pattern in an unconventional time signature becomes a central element. Minimalism can create a hypnotic effect.

EXPERIMENTING WITH MINIMALISM

Minimalism in music, characterized by simplicity, repetition, and a focus on subtle changes over time, is a compelling approach that can be explored effectively in guitar composition. Minimalist compositions often prioritize the interplay between musical elements, allowing listeners to engage with the nuances of repetition and gradual evolution.

Simplicity in Melody and Harmony:

Limit Musical Material: Embrace simplicity by using a limited set of melodic and harmonic elements. Minimalist compositions often thrive on the beauty found in the exploration of a few musical ideas.

Repetitive Motifs: Develop short, repetitive motifs that serve as the foundation for your composition. These motifs can be a series of chords, a short melodic phrase, or a rhythmic pattern.

Explore Repetition:

Cyclic Repetition: Experiment with cyclic repetition of musical elements. Repetition creates a hypnotic effect and allows listeners to delve into the subtleties of the composition.

Layered Repetition: Introduce layering by repeating different musical elements at various intervals. This creates depth and complexity within the minimalist framework.

Rhythmic Precision:

Focus on Rhythmic Patterns: Develop intricate rhythmic patterns that are repeated consistently. Pay attention to precision in your playing to maintain the rhythmic integrity of the composition.

Syncopation and Phrasing: Experiment with syncopated rhythms and varied phrasing within the repetition. This adds interest without deviating significantly from the minimalist ethos.

Use of Pulsating Patterns:

Create Pulsating Grooves: Establish a pulsating groove using repetitive patterns. This rhythmic foundation can be the heartbeat of your minimalist composition.

Dynamic Changes within Patterns: Introduce subtle dynamic changes within the repeating patterns to keep the listener engaged. This can involve variations in picking intensity, volume, or tonal qualities.

Modal Exploration:

Limitation to Modal Scales: Restrict your harmonic palette to modal scales, limiting the number of different notes and chords. This contributes to the overall simplicity and coherence of the composition.

Modal Interchange: Experiment with modal interchange within a minimalist framework.

Introducing a brief shift to a different mode can add a touch of complexity while maintaining a minimalist aesthetic.

Utilize Open Tunings and Drone Notes:

Open Tunings: Explore open tunings to create resonant, sustained sounds. Open tunings can facilitate the development of rich harmonic textures with minimal finger movement.

Drone Notes: Incorporate drone notes or pedal tones to add stability and continuity. A sustained drone can serve as a sonic anchor amidst repeated motifs.

Experiment with Looping Techniques:

Live Looping: Embrace live looping techniques to layer and build your composition in real-time. This allows you to play repetitive patterns and gradually introduce variations.

Pedalboard Effects: Utilize guitar effects pedals to create evolving textures. Experiment with delays, reverbs, and loopers to enhance the spatial and atmospheric qualities of your minimalist composition.

Dynamic Gradual Changes:

Subtle Dynamic Shifts: Introduce subtle dynamic changes over time. Gradual crescendos or decrescendos can add a sense of progression without deviating from the minimalist aesthetic.

Incorporate Crescendo and Diminuendo: Experiment with crescendo (building intensity) and diminuendo (diminishing intensity) techniques. These dynamic changes can be applied to individual notes or chords within repetitive patterns.

Silence as a Musical Element:

Strategic Pauses: Embrace silence as a crucial element in your minimalist composition. Strategic pauses can enhance the impact of repeated patterns and create moments of tension and release.

Rests and Breathing Space: Allow for breathing space between phrases. This gives listeners the opportunity to absorb the repetitive elements and appreciate the minimalist structure.

Experiment with Microtonality:

Microtonal Exploration: Explore microtonal intervals to introduce subtle pitch variations. This can add an unconventional and experimental dimension to your minimalist guitar composition.

Slide and Bend Techniques: Use slide and bend techniques to create microtonal shifts within repetitive motifs. This adds a touch of expressiveness while maintaining minimalist principles.

Example:

Consider a minimalist guitar composition where a simple two-chord progression is repeated cyclically. Within this repetition, experiment with varying picking patterns, dynamics, and the introduction of a sustained drone note. Gradually, the composition evolves by subtly altering the rhythmic patterns and introducing a slight shift in tonal color.

Exploring minimalist approaches in guitar composition invites you to embrace simplicity while experimenting with subtle variations over time. Whether through repetition, rhythmic precision, or dynamic changes, the minimalist ethos encourages a deep exploration of musical elements within a restrained framework.

As you delve into this style, you'll discover the beauty and expressiveness that can emerge from the artful repetition of a few carefully chosen musical ideas.

YOUR ARTISTIC INSTINCTS

Ultimately, trust your artistic instincts when selecting and experimenting with different time signatures. The goal is to enhance the rhythmic interest while maintaining the integrity of your musical vision.

Experimenting with different time signatures opens up a world of rhythmic possibilities for your guitar compositions. Embrace the diversity that various meters offer, and let the exploration of time signatures become a creative journey that adds depth and intrigue to your music.

TEMPO CHANGES

Decide where including tempo changes in your guitar composition would be effective.

DECIDING ON TEMPO CHANGES

Deciding whether to include tempo changes in your guitar composition is a significant artistic choice that can have a profound impact on the overall feel and dynamics of the music. Tempo changes add variety, tension, and a sense of movement to your composition.

THE ROLE OF TEMPO CHANGES

Familiarize yourself with the role that tempo changes can play in a composition. Tempo variations can evoke different emotions, highlight specific sections, and contribute to the overall narrative of the music.

Understanding the role of tempo changes in music is crucial for shaping the overall feel, energy, and emotional impact of a composition. Tempo, the speed at which a piece of music is performed, is a fundamental aspect of musical expression.

Common Tempo Markings:
Andante: At a walking pace, moderately slow.
Allegro: Fast, lively.
Adagio: Slow, leisurely.
Presto: Very fast.
BPM (Beats Per Minute): Tempo can be measured in beats per minute, providing a more precise indication

of speed. For example, a piece marked "120 BPM" suggests 120 beats in one minute.

Expressive Use of Tempo:

Mood and Emotion: Tempo significantly influences the mood and emotional character of a piece. Faster tempos may evoke excitement, urgency, or tension, while slower tempos can convey calmness, reflection, or sadness.

Dynamics: Tempo changes can be used dynamically to build intensity, create contrasts, and guide the listener through different emotional states within a composition.

Identifying Tempo Changes:

Notation: Tempo changes are often indicated by Italian terms (e.g., ritardando for slowing down, accelerando for speeding up) or specific metronome markings.

Musical Phrasing: Tempo changes can be embedded within the musical phrasing, marking transitions between sections, changes in mood, or climactic moments.

Gradual vs. Abrupt Changes:

Gradual Tempo Changes: Slow, gradual tempo changes are often used for subtle shifts in mood or to build tension gradually. These changes are marked by terms like ritardando or rallentando.

Abrupt Tempo Changes: Quick and sudden tempo changes, marked by terms like accelerando or stringendo, can create immediate shifts in energy and intensity.

Using Rubato:

Rubato Definition: Rubato is a tempo indication that allows for flexibility in the pacing of a piece. It involves borrowing time from one phrase and giving it back in another, creating a sense of expressive freedom.

Expressive Phrasing: Rubato is particularly effective in expressive genres like classical, jazz, or folk, where the tempo is subtly manipulated to emphasize certain phrases.

Role of Tempo in Different Genres:

Classical Music: Classical compositions often involve precise tempo markings and changes, with conductors interpreting the composer's intentions. Tempo plays a crucial role in conveying the composer's expressive and structural choices.

Jazz and Improvisational Music: Jazz often employs a flexible approach to tempo, allowing for improvisation. Musicians may engage in "rubato" and freely adjust the tempo to enhance expressiveness.

Rock and Pop: Popular music genres may feature consistent tempos within a song, but tempo changes can still be used for dramatic effect, especially during key transitions or in experimental genres.

Technical Considerations:

Guitar Technique: Tempo changes can impact the technical demands on guitarists. Faster tempos may require precise picking or strumming, while slower tempos allow for expressive phrasing and intricate fingerstyle work.

Metronome Practice: Practice with a metronome to develop a solid sense of time and control. Gradually increase or decrease the tempo to build technical proficiency.

Collaborative Considerations:

Communication with Musicians: In collaborative settings, clear communication about tempo changes is essential. Use musical terminology or discuss specific BPM values to ensure everyone is on the same page.

Feel and Groove: While tempo changes are precise, musicians often play with a certain "feel" or "groove" that goes beyond the metronomic tempo. Maintain a balance between precision and the natural flow of the music.

Recording and Listening:

Recording Practices: When recording, pay careful attention to tempo changes. Use the recording process to refine and adjust tempo nuances for optimal expressiveness.

Critical Listening: Listen critically to recordings of your compositions or performances. Evaluate the impact of tempo changes on the overall musical experience.

Experimentation and Artistic Expression:

Artistic Freedom: As a composer or performer, embrace the artistic freedom to experiment with tempo changes. Trust your intuition and explore how different tempos enhance the emotional narrative of your composition.

Innovation: Use tempo changes innovatively to distinguish your musical voice. Unconventional tempo shifts can be a signature element in your compositions.

Example:

Consider a guitar composition that begins with a slow and contemplative adagio section. As the piece progresses, it accelerates into an allegro section, introducing a sense of urgency and excitement. The tempo change enhances the contrast between the two sections, guiding the listener through distinct emotional landscapes.

Understanding the role of tempo changes in guitar composition is an essential aspect of musical expression. Whether used for dramatic effect, emotional nuance, or technical demands, tempo changes contribute significantly to the dynamic and expressive qualities of your music. Embrace the versatility of tempo as a tool for conveying your artistic intentions and creating a compelling musical journey for your audience.

MUSICAL CONTEXT AND TEMPO

Assess the musical context of your composition. Tempo changes are particularly effective in creating contrasts between sections or emphasizing key moments. Consider how tempo variations align with the mood and progression of your music.

CONSIDERING THE MUSICAL CONTEXT

Considering how tempo variations align with the mood and progression of your guitar composition is a key aspect of crafting a dynamic and emotionally resonant musical experience. Tempo changes play a crucial role in shaping the overall feel, energy, and narrative arc of your music.

Connect Tempo with Emotional Content:

Identify Emotional Peaks: Pinpoint moments in your composition where the emotional intensity peaks or changes. This could be during a climactic solo, a transition between sections, or a resolution in the harmony.

Match Tempo to Emotion: Adjust the tempo to align with the emotional content of each section. Faster tempos may heighten excitement, while slower tempos can evoke reflection or melancholy.

Gradual Tempo Shifts for Subtlety:

Subtle Mood Changes: Use gradual tempo shifts for subtle changes in mood. This approach is effective for creating nuanced emotional transitions without abrupt disruptions.

Transition Phrases: Introduce transitional phrases between sections with different tempos to guide listeners smoothly from one emotional landscape to another.

Accelerate for Intensity:

Building Tension: Accelerate the tempo during sections where tension is building. This creates a sense of urgency and anticipation, enhancing the intensity of the music.

Climactic Moments: Reserve faster tempos for climactic moments, such as the peak of a guitar solo or a powerful chord progression. The increased speed contributes to the overall impact.

Decelerate for Emphasis:

Emphasizing Melancholy or Contemplation: Decelerate the tempo for sections that require emphasis on melancholy, introspection, or contemplation. Slower tempos allow listeners to absorb and reflect on the emotional weight of the music.

Concluding Sections: Gradually decelerate towards the end of your composition to create a sense of closure. Slower tempos can provide a feeling of resolution and finality.

Tempo and Sectional Transitions:

Shifts between Sections: Use tempo changes to signal transitions between different sections of your composition. This can help define the structure of your piece and guide listeners through its narrative.

Distinctive Styles: Vary tempos to differentiate between stylistically distinct sections, such as moving from a fast-paced, rhythmic section to a slower, melodic one.

Coordinate with Dynamic Changes:

Dynamic Contrast: Align tempo changes with dynamic shifts in your guitar playing. For instance, when transitioning to a faster tempo, increase the intensity of your strumming or picking.

Build Gradually: Gradually build up the tempo in sections that require increased energy or excitement. This coordinated approach ensures a smooth and organic progression.

Experiment with Rubato:

Expressive Freedom: Utilize rubato for moments of expressive freedom. This technique allows you to temporarily stretch or compress time, enhancing the emotive qualities of your playing.

Rubato in Melodic Phrasing: Apply rubato in melodic phrasing, allowing certain notes or phrases to linger or hasten for added expressiveness.

Consider the Role of Percussion:

Percussive Elements in Guitar Playing: If incorporating percussive elements in your guitar playing, such as tapping or slapping, synchronize tempo changes with these rhythmic components to maintain cohesion.

Dynamics in Percussive Techniques: Adjust the dynamics of percussive techniques to complement changes in tempo. This creates a seamless blend of rhythmic and melodic elements.

Create a Tempo Map:

Plan and Visualize: Develop a tempo map for your composition. This visual representation helps you plan where tempo changes occur and visualize their alignment with the mood and progression of the music.

Digital Audio Workstations (DAWs): If using a DAW, utilize tempo automation to precisely control tempo changes. This allows you to experiment and refine the timing of tempo shifts.

Consider Genre Characteristics:

Adapt to Genre Dynamics: Consider the conventions of the genre you're working within. Some genres naturally incorporate frequent tempo changes, while others may benefit from subtler shifts.

Experiment in Fusion Genres: In fusion genres, where multiple influences converge, explore creative combinations of tempos to create a unique and eclectic sound.

Example:

Imagine a guitar composition that begins with a slow and contemplative section, expressing a sense of introspection. As the piece progresses, it moves into a faster tempo during a lively and rhythmic chorus, conveying excitement. Towards the end, the tempo gradually decelerates, providing a calm and reflective conclusion.

Understanding how tempo variations align with the mood and progression of your guitar composition allows you to harness the full expressive potential of your music. By thoughtfully integrating tempo changes, you can guide listeners through a dynamic and emotionally engaging journey.

Whether creating tension, emphasizing climactic moments, or enhancing reflective passages, the strategic use of tempo variations contributes to the overall impact and resonance of your guitar compositions.

EMOTIONAL IMPACT AND TEMPO CHANGES

Determine the emotional impact you want to achieve in different sections of your composition. Tempo changes can heighten intensity, create anticipation, or provide moments of repose. Consider where these emotional shifts would be most effective.

EMOTIONAL RESONANCE AND TEMPO

The tempo of a guitar composition is a powerful expressive tool that significantly influences the emotional impact of the music. The speed at which a piece is played can evoke various emotions, set the mood, and shape the overall listening experience.

Energizing and Exciting:

Fast Tempos: Higher tempos, such as allegro or presto, create a sense of energy and excitement. Fast-paced guitar playing can evoke feelings of exhilaration and drive.

Example: Upbeat and energetic guitar compositions with rapid picking or strumming patterns can convey joy, enthusiasm, or even a sense of adventure.

Uplifting and Optimistic:

Moderate Tempos: Moderate tempos, like andante or moderato, often contribute to an uplifting and optimistic feel. These tempos provide a balance between energy and a sense of stability.

Example: A guitar piece played at a moderate tempo with uplifting chord progressions can evoke feelings of hope, positivity, or contentment.

Reflective and Contemplative:

Slow Tempos: Slower tempos, such as adagio or largo, create a contemplative and reflective atmosphere. The deliberate pacing allows listeners to absorb and reflect on the emotional nuances.

Example: A slow, melodic guitar composition with expressive phrasing can convey introspection, nostalgia, or a sense of deep emotion.

Tension and Urgency:

Gradual Acceleration: A gradual increase in tempo can build tension and urgency, heightening emotional impact. This technique is often used to lead into climactic moments.

Example: A guitar composition that starts slow and gradually accelerates can create a sense of anticipation, leading to a dramatic and intense section.

Dramatic Shifts:

Abrupt Tempo Changes: Abrupt shifts in tempo can introduce dramatic contrasts, impacting the emotional landscape of the composition. These shifts can surprise and captivate the listener.

Example: A sudden transition from a slow ballad to a fast-paced section can create a dynamic and emotionally charged effect.

Expressive Rubato:

Flexible Timing: The use of rubato, where the tempo is temporarily slowed down or accelerated for expressive purposes, allows for emotional nuances.

Rubato provides a sense of freedom and emotional expression.

Example: Applying rubato to a melodic phrase in a guitar solo can add a touch of emotive expression and connect with the listener on a more personal level.

Matching Emotional Themes:

Alignment with Lyrics or Themes: Aligning the tempo with the emotional themes conveyed by lyrics or an overarching musical concept enhances the coherence and impact of the composition.

Example: If the lyrics of a song tell a story of overcoming challenges, a gradually increasing tempo can symbolize the triumph and resilience within the narrative.

Genre-specific Impact:

Genre Conventions: Different genres have specific tempo conventions that listeners associate with certain emotions. Adhering to or subverting these expectations can influence the emotional impact.

Example: In blues music, a slow tempo is often associated with soulful, heartfelt expressions, while in punk rock, a fast tempo may convey a sense of rebellion and intensity.

Cinematic Quality:

Film Score Influence: Tempos in guitar compositions can emulate the pacing found in film scores. Using slower tempos for poignant moments and faster tempos for action sequences can create a cinematic quality.

Example: Composing a guitar piece with varying tempos to accompany a visual narrative can enhance the emotional impact, much like in a film soundtrack.

Dynamic Interaction with Other Instruments:

Ensemble Dynamics: The tempo of a guitar composition interacts with other instruments in an ensemble, influencing the collective emotional impact. Cohesive tempo decisions enhance the overall emotional coherence.

Example: In a band setting, synchronizing tempos between guitars, drums, and other instruments ensures a unified emotional expression.

The tempo of a guitar composition is a dynamic and versatile element that shapes the emotional experience for both the musician and the listener. By thoughtfully selecting and manipulating tempos, a guitarist can convey a wide range of emotions, creating a profound and memorable musical journey. Whether aiming for excitement, reflection, tension, or expressive freedom, understanding the emotional impact of tempo choices is essential for crafting a compelling and evocative guitar composition.

GRADUAL AND ABRUPT CHANGES

Experiment with gradual tempo changes. Gradual accelerandos or ritardandos can create a subtle sense of motion and are often well-suited for transitional passages.

EXPERIMENTING WITH CHANGES

The impact of gradual and abrupt changes in tempo is a nuanced and expressive aspect of guitar composition. The choice between gradual and abrupt tempo changes significantly influences the emotional and dynamic character of the music.

GRADUAL CHANGES IN TEMPO

Building Tension:

Impact: Gradual tempo changes are effective for building tension and anticipation. They allow the listener to feel the increasing energy and momentum within a section.

Example: In a guitar solo, a gradual accelerando can build tension, leading to a climactic moment.

Smooth Transitions:

Impact: Gradual tempo changes facilitate smooth transitions between sections, maintaining a coherent flow in the music.

Example: Transitioning from a slow, melodic verse to an energetic chorus can be achieved with a gradual accelerando.

Expressive Rubato:

Impact: The use of rubato, a form of expressive freedom in tempo, often involves gradual changes. It adds a human touch and allows for emotional expression.

Example: Applying rubato to a delicate guitar phrase in a ballad can create a sense of vulnerability and intimacy.

Climactic Build-ups:

Impact: Gradual accelerations can be employed to build up to climactic moments, enhancing the emotional impact of the composition.

Example: Gradually increasing the tempo before a powerful chord progression or solo can heighten the sense of drama.

Reflective Slowdowns:

Impact: Gradual ritardandos or slow-downs are effective for conveying introspection and creating a more relaxed, reflective mood.

Example: Slowing down the tempo towards the end of a piece can create a calming effect, providing a sense of resolution.

ABRUPT CHANGES IN TEMPO:

Dramatic Contrasts:

Impact: Abrupt changes in tempo create sudden and dramatic contrasts, capturing the listener's attention and adding excitement.

Example: Shifting from a slow, melancholic section to a fast-paced, rhythmic passage can create a dynamic contrast.

Surprise and Impact:

Impact: Abrupt tempo changes can surprise the listener, injecting unpredictability into the composition and keeping the music engaging.

Example: Suddenly speeding up the tempo after a period of slower playing can catch the audience off guard, adding an element of surprise.

Expressive Agitation:

Impact: Abrupt accelerandos can convey a sense of urgency or agitation, adding intensity to the music.

Example: A sudden increase in tempo during a guitar solo can inject a burst of energy and excitement.

Dynamic Shifts between Sections:

Impact: Abrupt tempo changes are effective for delineating distinct sections of a composition, emphasizing shifts in mood or style.

Example: Transitioning from a fast-paced, intricate guitar riff to a slow, melodic interlude creates a clear boundary between sections.

Experimental and Avant-Garde Effects:

Impact: In experimental genres, abrupt tempo changes are embraced for avant-garde effects, pushing the boundaries of traditional musical structures.

Example: Abruptly switching between different tempos in a progressive metal composition can contribute to its complex and innovative sound.

COMBINED APPROACH

Blend of Gradual and Abrupt:

Impact: Combining both gradual and abrupt tempo changes allows for a dynamic and diverse musical experience, offering moments of both continuity and contrast.

Example: A composition may gradually accelerate in intensity before suddenly dropping to a slower tempo for a brief, contemplative interlude.

Genre Adaptation:

Impact: The choice between gradual and abrupt changes often depends on the genre. Some genres favor one approach over the other, and adapting to genre conventions can enhance the overall impact.

Example: In jazz, gradual tempo changes during improvisational sections are common, while certain progressive rock compositions may feature abrupt shifts for avant-garde effects.

The impact of gradual and abrupt changes in tempo for guitar composition lies in their ability to shape the emotional narrative and dynamics of the music. The choice between gradual and abrupt shifts depends on the desired emotional impact and the stylistic context of the composition.

DYNAMICS AND TEMPO CHANGES

Coordinate tempo changes with dynamic changes. For example, a crescendo leading into a faster tempo can intensify the emotional impact of a section.

COORDINATE TEMPO AND DYNAMIC CHANGES

Coordinating tempo changes with dynamic changes in a guitar composition is a powerful technique that enhances the overall expressiveness and impact of the music. The interplay between tempo and dynamics contributes to the emotional nuances and narrative flow of the composition.

Understand the Relationship:

Tempo-Dynamic Symbiosis: Recognize that tempo and dynamics are symbiotic elements. Changes in tempo can influence the perceived intensity, and dynamic shifts can complement alterations in tempo.

Map Out Musical Phrases:

Identify Key Phrases: Break down your composition into distinct musical phrases or sections where dynamic and tempo changes are appropriate.

Align Gradual Changes:

Gradual Dynamics and Tempo: For gradual changes, coordinate a gradual increase in dynamics with a simultaneous accelerando or ritardando.

Example: As you build up to a climax, gradually increase both the tempo and dynamic intensity.

Highlight Dynamic Peaks:

Matching Dynamics to Tempo Peaks: Ensure that dynamic peaks align with tempo peaks to emphasize climactic moments in your composition.

Example: A powerful guitar solo may be both dynamically and tempo-wise intense, creating a focal point in the composition.

Experiment with Dynamic Gradations:

Nuanced Dynamics: Within a single tempo section, experiment with nuanced dynamics to convey subtleties in emotion.

Example: In a slow, melodic passage, use a crescendo to gradually increase the volume, adding emotional depth.

Contrast with Abrupt Changes:

Abrupt Dynamics and Tempo Contrasts: For abrupt changes, synchronize sudden dynamic shifts with immediate tempo changes for a striking contrast.

Example: Going from a quiet, contemplative section to a loud and fast-paced segment creates a dynamic and tempo-related contrast.

Expressive Rubato Moments:

Rubato Dynamics: In rubato sections where the tempo is flexible, match changes in dynamics to the ebb and flow of the expressive phrasing.

Example: During a rubato guitar solo, the dynamics may rise and fall organically with the guitarist's expressive interpretation.

Use Tempo Modulation for Dynamics:

Tempo Modulation Techniques: Explore tempo modulation techniques, such as ritardando leading to a quieter section or accelerando preceding a louder segment.

Example: A gradual slowdown in tempo can lead into a softer, more delicate guitar passage.

Integrate Percussive Dynamics:

Percussive Elements: If incorporating percussive techniques in your guitar playing, synchronize dynamic accents with changes in tempo to enhance rhythmic impact.

Example: A sudden increase in dynamic emphasis on percussive strumming may coincide with a tempo acceleration for heightened rhythmic intensity.

Consider Genre Dynamics:

Genre-specific Considerations: Different genres have conventions regarding the coordination of dynamics and tempo. Be aware of these conventions and adapt accordingly.

Example: In flamenco guitar, dynamic changes often align with shifts in tempo, emphasizing the rhythmic and emotional impact.

Practice with a Metronome:

Metronome Practice: Use a metronome during practice to precisely coordinate dynamic changes with specific beats or subdivisions, ensuring accuracy in tempo shifts.

Example: Practice a section where the dynamic intensity increases with each beat of the metronome, creating a dynamic build-up.

Embrace Experimentation:

Artistic Freedom: Allow for experimentation and artistic freedom. Not every dynamic shift needs to correlate with a change in tempo, but understanding when to align them enhances your expressive palette.

Example: An experimental section may feature unexpected dynamics that don't strictly follow the tempo, creating a unique sonic landscape.

Example:

Consider a guitar composition with a quiet and reflective introduction. As the composition progresses, it transitions into a faster-paced section with an accelerando, reaching a dynamic climax during a solo. The return to a slower tempo in the concluding section coincides with a gradual diminuendo, creating a sense of resolution and tranquility.

Coordinating tempo changes with dynamic changes in a guitar composition requires careful consideration of the emotional impact you want to convey. By aligning these elements thoughtfully, you create a more immersive and engaging musical experience for your audience. The dynamic interplay between tempo and dynamics adds depth, drama, and emotional resonance to your guitar compositions.

TIME SIGNATURE AND TEMPO

If your composition includes changes in time signature, align tempo changes with these shifts. Coordinated changes enhance the overall rhythmic complexity and impact.

ALIGNING WITH CHANGES IN TIME SIGNATURE

Aligning with changes in time signature is an essential skill for any musician, particularly in the context of guitar composition. Time signature changes can add complexity, dynamics, and a unique character to your music. When adjusting to these changes, it's crucial to consider how they affect the overall tempo development of your composition.

Understand the Time Signature Changes:
Before delving into tempo adjustments, ensure you thoroughly understand the time signature changes in your composition. Different time signatures can affect the feel and flow of your music, so be aware of the rhythmic patterns associated with each signature.

Map Out the Structure:
Create a clear roadmap of your composition, highlighting sections where time signature changes occur. Understanding the structure will help you anticipate shifts in tempo and plan your guitar parts accordingly.

Transition Smoothly:

Smooth transitions between time signatures are crucial for maintaining the overall flow of your composition. Practice transitioning between sections with different time signatures to ensure a seamless shift in tempo. Use metronomes or drum tracks to help you stay in time during these transitions.

Tempo Mapping:

Consider creating a tempo map for your composition, indicating the tempo at different points where time signature changes occur. This map serves as a reference for both your practice sessions and recording, ensuring that you maintain the desired pace throughout the piece.

Metronome Practice:

Practice with a metronome to develop a strong sense of timing. Start by playing your composition at a slower tempo and gradually increase the speed as you become more comfortable with the transitions. This methodical approach helps you internalize the changes in time signature.

Dynamic Phrasing:

Explore how changes in time signature can influence your guitar phrasing and dynamics. Experiment with different rhythmic patterns and accents that complement the new time signature, adding depth and character to your composition.

Utilize Syncopation:

Syncopation can be a powerful tool when aligning with changes in time signature. Experiment with offbeat accents and syncopated rhythms to create interesting and engaging guitar parts that enhance the overall musical experience.

Record and Analyze:

Record yourself playing the composition and analyze the playback. Pay attention to how well you align with the changes in time signature and whether the tempo transitions are smooth. Recording allows you to identify areas that need improvement and refine your performance.

Collaborate with a Metronome or Backing Track:

Collaborating with a metronome or a backing track that follows the changing time signatures can be beneficial. It provides a solid rhythmic foundation, helping you stay on track and ensuring a consistent tempo development.

Experiment and Innovate:

Don't be afraid to experiment with unconventional time signatures or tempo changes. Pushing boundaries can lead to unique and compelling musical compositions. Embrace creativity while maintaining a balance that suits the overall mood of your piece.

Aligning with changes in time signature for tempo development in guitar composition requires a combination of understanding, practice, and creativity. By mastering these elements, you can create captivating compositions that showcase your musical prowess and captivate your audience.

RITARDANDO AND ACCELERANDO

Experiment with ritardandos (slowing down) or accelerandos (speeding up) in specific passages. These gradual tempo changes can add a nuanced sense of motion and expression.

EXPERIMENTING WITH RITARDANDO OR ACCELERANDO

Experimenting with ritardando (slowing down) and accelerando (speeding up) is a fantastic way to add expressive and dynamic elements to your guitar compositions. These tempo variations can evoke emotion, create tension, and contribute to the overall musicality of your piece.

RITARDANDO

Gradual Slowdown:

Gradually decrease the tempo over a few measures, leading to a ritardando. This can build anticipation and add a dramatic touch to the composition. Experiment with slowing down evenly or more pronouncedly towards the end of a section.

Example: The ending of *Stairway to Heaven* by Led Zeppelin features a gradual ritardando, enhancing the emotional impact of the closing guitar solo.

Rubato Technique:

Utilize rubato, a flexible tempo where certain notes or phrases are played freely. This technique allows you to stretch or compress time, adding a sense of freedom and expression.

Example: In *Blackbird* by The Beatles, Paul McCartney uses rubato to create a flowing and emotive guitar arrangement.

Use of Crescendo:

Combine ritardando with a crescendo (gradual increase in volume) for a powerful effect. This builds tension as both tempo and intensity decrease simultaneously.

Example: The guitar solo in *Comfortably Numb* by Pink Floyd features a beautiful ritardando accompanied by a crescendo, contributing to the emotional climax of the solo.

ACCELERANDO

Build Energy with Crescendo:

Start with a moderate tempo and gradually increase speed, coupled with a crescendo. This technique is excellent for building energy and excitement in your composition.

Example: The instrumental section in *Bohemian Rhapsody* by Queen accelerates dramatically, adding intensity to the guitar-driven climax.

Unexpected Speed Changes:

Introduce unexpected accelerandos to catch the listener off guard. This can create a sense of unpredictability and keep the audience engaged.

Example: In *Layla* by Derek and the Dominos, the famous guitar coda features unexpected accelerandos, enhancing the emotional impact of the section.

Syncopated Acceleration:

Experiment with syncopated patterns in your accelerando, introducing rhythmic complexity. This can add a dynamic and lively feel to your guitar composition.

Example: *Money for Nothing* by Dire Straits incorporates syncopated accelerandos in the guitar riffs, contributing to the energetic feel of the song.

COMBINED RITARDANDO AND ACCELERANDO

Transitioning Between Sections:

Use ritardando to smoothly transition between sections, and then introduce accelerando to propel the composition forward. This creates a dynamic contrast between different parts of your piece.

Example: The instrumental break in *Hotel California* by Eagles features a combination of ritardando and accelerando, creating a captivating transition between the mellow and intense sections.

Create a Climactic Ending:

Combine both ritardando and accelerando to build up to a climactic ending. This technique is powerful in creating a memorable and emotionally charged conclusion.

Example: The final guitar solo in *November Rain* by Guns N' Roses employs a combination of ritardando and accelerando, contributing to the epic feel of the closing moments.

Incorporating ritardando and accelerando into your guitar compositions allows you to showcase your creativity and evoke a wide range of emotions. By studying these examples from popular music, you can gain inspiration for implementing tempo variations in your own unique way.

Experimentation is key, so don't hesitate to explore different approaches until you find what resonates best with the mood and style of your composition.

CONCLUDING WITH RITARDANDO

Consider ending your composition with a ritardando for a gradual deceleration, creating a sense of resolution and closure.

CONSIDER RITARDANDO AT THE END

Considering ritardando at the end of a guitar composition can be a powerful and expressive choice that enhances the overall emotional impact of the piece. Ritardando, or a gradual slowing down of tempo, serves to create a sense of closure, drama, and finality.

Emotional Resolution:

Ritardando provides a natural and emotive way to bring a composition to a close. Slowing down the tempo can evoke a sense of resolution, allowing the listener to absorb the emotions conveyed throughout the piece.

Example: In *Classical Gas* by Mason Williams, the closing section features a gentle ritardando, contributing to the emotional resolution and providing a satisfying conclusion to the intricate guitar arrangement.

Enhanced Dramatic Effect:

Gradually slowing down the tempo builds tension and drama, making the conclusion of your composition more impactful. It can create a climactic moment that leaves a lasting impression on the listener.

Example: The ending of *Dust in the Wind* by Kansas incorporates a ritardando, adding a poignant touch to the acoustic guitar arpeggios and enhancing the dramatic effect of the closing chords.

Highlighting the Final Chord:

Ritardando allows you to emphasize the final chord or notes of your composition. This can give the listener a moment to savor the resolution and appreciate the beauty of the concluding musical phrase.

Example: *Hotel California* by Eagles concludes with a gradual ritardando, accentuating the final chord and contributing to the overall impact of the iconic guitar outro.

Smooth Transition to Silence:

Slowing down the tempo at the end provides a smooth transition to silence, allowing the music to fade away gracefully. This technique is particularly effective in acoustic and intimate settings.

Example: In *Tears in Heaven* by Eric Clapton, the final chords are accompanied by a subtle ritardando, creating a poignant transition to silence and emphasizing the contemplative mood of the song.

Creating a Memorable Ending:

A ritardando at the end can make your composition more memorable. By giving the listener a moment to reflect on the musical journey, you leave a lasting impression that resonates beyond the final notes.

Example: *Wonderful Tonight* by Eric Clapton concludes with a gentle ritardando, contributing to the tender and romantic atmosphere of the song and creating a memorable ending.

Expressive Variability:

Ritardando provides an opportunity for expressive variability in your compositions. It allows you to showcase the emotional depth of your playing and connect with the audience on a more profound level.

Example: The outro of *Wish You Were Here* by Pink Floyd features a subtle ritardando, enhancing the melancholic and introspective mood of the song and adding expressive variability to the closing moments.

In summary, considering ritardando at the end of a guitar composition can be a deliberate and effective choice for achieving emotional resolution, enhancing dramatic impact, and creating a memorable conclusion. By studying examples from various genres and incorporating this technique into your own compositions, you can add a nuanced and expressive dimension to your guitar playing.

TECHNICAL DEMANDS AND TEMPO

Take into account the technical demands on the guitar and your playing style. Ensure that tempo changes are feasible and enhance the musicality without compromising execution.

Thinking About Technical Demands

Ensuring that tempo changes in your guitar composition are both feasible and enhance musicality is crucial for delivering a performance that captivates listeners without compromising execution.

Gradual Transitions:

Implement gradual transitions when changing tempos. Abrupt shifts can be challenging for both the performer and the audience to follow. Gradual changes provide a smoother experience and allow for better adaptability.

Practice with a Metronome:

Use a metronome during practice to develop a solid sense of timing. This is essential for maintaining consistency during tempo changes. Practice gradually increasing or decreasing the tempo at the specific points where changes occur.

Establish Clear Cue Points:

Clearly mark cue points for tempo changes in your composition. This can be achieved through visual cues in the sheet music or mental landmarks within the piece. Knowing when to anticipate a tempo change helps in executing it seamlessly.

Maintain Control:

As a guitarist, it's crucial to maintain control over your playing, especially during tempo changes. Be mindful of your picking hand, finger movements, and fretting accuracy. A controlled technique ensures that your execution remains precise even when adjusting the tempo.

Consider Technical Ability:

Assess your technical ability and the technical demands of your composition. Ensure that tempo changes align with your skill level and that you can execute them comfortably. Pushing beyond your technical limits may compromise the overall quality of your performance.

Use Tempo Changes Purposefully:

Implement tempo changes with a clear musical purpose. Avoid unnecessary fluctuations that may disrupt the flow of the composition. Every tempo change should contribute to the overall emotional and artistic expression of the piece.

Experiment with Subtle Variations:

Explore subtle variations in tempo to add nuance without introducing significant challenges. Micro-dynamic changes can enhance musicality without creating difficulties in execution. Experiment with slight accelerandos or ritardandos to see how they impact the overall feel of the composition.

Collaborate with Backing Tracks:

Practice with backing tracks that include tempo changes. This simulates a real performance environment and helps you adapt to varying tempos. It also allows you to assess your ability to synchronize with external cues.

Record and Analyze:

Record yourself playing the composition and analyze the playback. Pay attention to how well you execute the tempo changes and whether they enhance the musicality. Recording provides valuable insights into areas that may need improvement.

Seek Feedback:

Share your composition with fellow musicians or mentors and seek feedback on the feasibility and musicality of the tempo changes. External perspectives can offer valuable insights and help refine your approach.

Consider Live Performance Challenges:

If your composition is intended for live performance, consider the challenges of executing tempo changes on stage. Factors such as nerves, different acoustics, and potential distractions should be taken into account during the composition and rehearsal stages.

Rehearse at Performance Speed:

Practice your composition at the intended performance speed regularly. This ensures that you are comfortable with the tempo changes and can execute them reliably in a live setting.

By incorporating these considerations into your approach to tempo changes in guitar composition, you can strike a balance between musicality and feasibility, ensuring that your performance is both expressive and technically sound.

RUBATO AND TEMPO CHANGES

Experiment with rubato, a flexible approach to tempo where the speed of the music ebbs and flows. Rubato can be particularly effective in expressive and emotive passages.

EXPERIMENTING WITH RUBATO

Rubato is a term in music that literally means "robbed" in Italian. It refers to a flexible and expressive interpretation of tempo where the musician takes liberties with the rhythm, slowing down or speeding up certain passages for artistic effect. Rubato allows for a more emotional and personalized performance, creating a sense of freedom within the musical expression.

USE OF RUBATO IN EXPRESSIVE PASSAGES

Expressive Phrasing:

Rubato is particularly effective in expressive and emotive passages of a guitar composition. It allows the guitarist to shape phrases with nuance, emphasizing certain notes or moments for added emotional impact. This freedom in timing contributes to a more fluid and personalized interpretation.

Example: In classical guitar compositions, such as pieces by Francisco Tárrega or Fernando Sor, rubato is often employed to bring out the lyrical and emotive qualities of the music. The guitarist might linger on a poignant melody, creating a sense of introspection and emotional depth.

Enhancing Melodic Lines:

Rubato can be used to enhance the natural ebb and flow of melodic lines. By stretching or compressing time in specific places, the guitarist can draw attention to the melodic peaks and valleys, creating a more compelling narrative within the composition.

Example: In fingerstyle arrangements, like those by Tommy Emmanuel or Chet Atkins, rubato is used to accentuate the melodic intricacies. The guitarist might linger on a climactic note or subtly quicken the pace to add tension before a resolution.

Emotional Intensity:

Rubato allows for the injection of emotional intensity into a composition. By momentarily slowing down or speeding up, the guitarist can convey a heightened sense of emotion, making the performance more engaging and evocative.

Example: Consider the use of rubato in the iconic guitar solos of David Gilmour in Pink Floyd's *Comfortably Numb*. The expressive bends and pauses created by rubato contribute to the intense and emotional impact of the solo.

Mimicking Vocal Expression:

Rubato is often employed to mimic the natural expressiveness of human vocals. In passages where the guitar is meant to emulate the human voice, rubato can add a vocal-like quality, allowing the guitarist to breathe life into the music.

Example: In acoustic singer-songwriter compositions, artists like James Taylor use rubato to convey the intimate and personal nature of their lyrics. The guitarist might stretch time during poignant phrases, enhancing the emotional delivery.

Creating Moments of Tension and Release:

Rubato is an effective tool for creating moments of tension and release within a composition. By momentarily disrupting the regular pulse, the guitarist can build anticipation before resolving back to a stable tempo.

Example: Jazz guitarists, such as Joe Pass, often employ rubato during improvisational sections. The guitarist might use rubato to build tension before launching into a fast and virtuosic run, creating a sense of release and excitement.

In conclusion, rubato is a powerful expressive tool in guitar composition. When used thoughtfully in expressive and emotive passages, it adds a unique character to the music, allowing the guitarist to infuse their performance with personality, emotion, and a sense of storytelling. The careful application of rubato can elevate a composition, making it more memorable and resonant to the listener.

EXPRESSIVE PHRASING AND TEMPO

Align tempo changes with expressive phrasing. Adjusting the tempo to complement the rise and fall of melodic lines or thematic material enhances the overall musicality.

ALIGN WITH EXPRESSIVE PHRASING

Aligning tempo changes with expressive phrasing is a nuanced and effective way to enhance the emotive qualities of your guitar composition. This approach allows you to synchronize the rhythmic shifts with the musical content, creating a more cohesive and engaging listening experience.

Identify Key Expressive Phrases:
Begin by identifying the sections of your composition where expressive phrasing is essential. These are moments that carry emotional weight, such as melodic peaks, climaxes, or passages with intense dynamics.

Understand the Emotional Intent:
Delve into the emotional intent behind each expressive phrase. Consider whether the phrasing calls for a slowdown to convey introspection, or if an acceleration might heighten the sense of excitement and intensity.

Map Out Phrasing Variations:
Map out variations in your expressive phrasing to align with tempo changes. Determine where you want

to stretch time for added emphasis and where you might quicken the pace to create a sense of urgency or excitement.

Practice Phrasing within Tempo Changes:

Practice playing the expressive phrases within the context of tempo changes. Use a metronome or backing track to simulate the changing rhythmic landscape and ensure that your expressive phrasing remains synchronized.

Experiment with Rubato:

Introduce rubato during expressive phrasing to emphasize certain notes or phrases. Experiment with subtle slowing down or speeding up to add nuance and depth to the emotive content.

Use Tempo Modulation Techniques:

Explore tempo modulation techniques such as ritardando (gradual slowing down), accelerando (gradual speeding up), or fermata (pausing on a note). Apply these techniques strategically to align with expressive phrasing.

Employ Dynamic Contrasts:

Introduce dynamic contrasts along with tempo changes. Consider increasing volume as you accelerate or decreasing it during a ritardando to amplify the expressive impact of your phrasing.

Align with Harmonic Changes:

If there are harmonic changes accompanying your expressive phrasing, coordinate tempo changes accordingly. This ensures that both the rhythmic and harmonic dimensions of your composition work together seamlessly.

Consider Articulation and Technique:

Pay attention to articulation and technique within expressive phrasing. For instance, you might choose to use legato techniques during slower tempos and staccato or accentuated picking during faster tempos for added articulative expression.

Evaluate Natural Musical Flow:

Assess the natural flow of your composition, considering whether the tempo changes and expressive phrasing contribute positively to the overall musical narrative. Ensure that the alignment feels organic and enhances the listener's experience.

Record and Listen Critically:

Record your composition and listen critically to the playback. Evaluate how well the tempo changes align with expressive phrasing, and identify any areas where adjustments may be needed for better synchronization.

Seek Feedback:

Share your composition with others, seeking feedback specifically on how the alignment of tempo changes with expressive phrasing enhances or detracts from the overall musicality. External perspectives can provide valuable insights.

By carefully aligning tempo changes with expressive phrasing, you create a more dynamic and emotionally resonant guitar composition. This approach allows you to shape the narrative of your music, guiding the listener through a rich and engaging musical experience.

TEMPO CHANGES AS STRUCTURAL ELEMENT

Integrate tempo changes as a structural element in your composition. Define specific sections or themes by associating them with distinct tempos.

DEFINING AND DIFFERENTIATING SECTIONS THROUGH TEMPO

Defining specific sections or themes in a guitar composition by associating them with distinct tempos is a powerful way to create contrast, highlight musical ideas, and contribute to the overall structure of the piece.

Identify Musical Themes or Sections:

Begin by identifying distinct musical themes or sections within your composition. These could be characterized by changes in melody, harmony, rhythm, dynamics, or overall mood.

Consider Emotional Context:

Think about the emotional context of each section. Consider whether a particular theme conveys a sense of excitement, introspection, tension, or resolution. The emotional content can guide your choice of tempo.

Choose Tempos that Reflect Themes:

Select tempos that align with the musical and emotional characteristics of each theme. Faster tempos might suit energetic or lively sections, while slower tempos can enhance the expressiveness of more contemplative themes.

Gradual Transitions Between Themes:

If your composition involves transitioning between distinct themes, consider using gradual tempo changes to make the transitions smooth. Gradual transitions help maintain coherence and guide the listener through the musical journey.

Experiment with Time Signatures:

Explore different time signatures for each theme to further distinguish them. A change in time signature often accompanies a shift in tempo, creating a clear and recognizable boundary between sections.

Dynamic Contrasts:

Use dynamic contrasts alongside tempo changes to emphasize the differences between themes. For example, a shift from a slow tempo to a fast tempo can be accompanied by an increase in volume, adding impact to the transition.

Utilize Rubato for Phrasing:

Within each theme, consider using rubato or tempo flexibility to enhance expressive phrasing. This adds a layer of nuance to each section, even if the overall tempo remains constant.

EXAMPLES

Classical Guitar Composition:

In a classical guitar piece, such as Fernando Sor's *Grand Solo*, the composition might start with a slow and majestic theme (Adagio) characterized by a moderate tempo. As it progresses, it transitions to a lively and virtuosic theme (Allegro) with a faster tempo, defining a clear shift in mood and intensity.

Flamenco Guitar Piece:

In a flamenco guitar composition, a *Soleá* section might be played at a moderate tempo, showcasing intricate melodic patterns. This can transition into a *Bulería* section with a faster tempo, introducing dynamic rhythmic variations and a more upbeat atmosphere.

Fingerstyle Acoustic Composition:

In a fingerstyle acoustic composition, a reflective and melodic section might be played at a slower tempo, creating a contemplative mood. This can lead to a contrasting section with a faster tempo, featuring percussive elements and intricate fingerpicking patterns.

Rock Guitar Solo:

In a rock guitar solo, a melodic and expressive theme might be played at a moderate tempo, emphasizing sustained notes and bends. This can lead to a faster tempo during a shredding or virtuosic theme, adding intensity and showcasing technical prowess.

Jazz Guitar Composition:

In a jazz guitar composition, a laid-back swing section might feature a moderate tempo, allowing for expressive phrasing and improvisation. This can transition to a bebop-influenced section with a faster tempo, highlighting intricate and fast-paced lines.

University Scholastic Press

Remember that the key is to use tempo changes purposefully to define sections, create contrast, and convey the intended emotional and musical narrative of your composition. Careful consideration of tempos can elevate the overall impact of your guitar composition and engage the listener in a dynamic musical journey.

GENRE AND TEMPO CHANGES

Consider the genre of your composition. Certain genres, like progressive rock or classical, often embrace and even demand tempo changes as part of their stylistic conventions.

Considering The Genre

Several musical genres embrace and often demand tempo changes as part of their stylistic conventions for guitar composition. These changes contribute to the unique characteristics and expressive qualities of each genre.

.Jazz:

Jazz is known for its improvisational nature and dynamic tempo changes. In jazz guitar compositions, musicians often incorporate accelerandos, ritardandos, and sudden shifts in tempo to add excitement and spontaneity.

Example: *Take Five* by Dave Brubeck is a classic jazz piece that features a distinctive 5/4 time signature and explores various tempo changes, creating a dynamic and engaging listening experience.

Progressive Rock:

Progressive rock is characterized by its complexity, intricate arrangements, and experimentation. Guitar compositions in this genre frequently incorporate tempo changes to navigate through diverse musical landscapes, often within a single piece.

Example: *Roundabout* by Yes is a progressive rock classic that features intricate guitar work and frequent tempo changes, contributing to the genre's progressive and experimental nature.

Metal:

Various subgenres of metal, such as progressive metal and technical death metal, often incorporate complex tempo changes. Rapid shifts between fast and slow tempos contribute to the intensity and technicality of metal guitar compositions.

Example: *Dance of Eternity* by Dream Theater is an instrumental piece that showcases the band's technical prowess, featuring numerous tempo changes and intricate guitar passages.

Fusion:

Fusion blends elements of jazz, rock, and other genres, and it frequently involves tempo changes to create a dynamic and eclectic sound. Fusion guitar compositions may transition seamlessly between different tempos, showcasing versatility and creativity.

Example: *Birdland* by Weather Report is a fusion classic that features energetic guitar passages and explores various tempo changes within the context of the overall composition.

Flamenco:

Flamenco, a traditional Spanish music genre, often incorporates rhythmic complexities and tempo changes. Flamenco guitar compositions may include shifts between fast-paced, rhythmic sections and slower, melodic passages.

Example: *Entre Dos Aguas* by Paco de Lucía is a flamenco masterpiece that showcases the guitarist's virtuosity and features tempo changes between the rhythmic "bulería" and the more melodic "soleá."

Latin Jazz:

Latin jazz, influenced by Afro-Cuban and Brazilian rhythms, often involves intricate percussive elements and rhythmic variations. Guitar compositions in this genre may include tempo changes to accommodate the diverse rhythmic patterns.

Example: *Black Orpheus (Manhã de Carnaval)* is a Latin jazz standard often adapted for guitar. It incorporates tempo changes to reflect the shifting moods and rhythms associated with Brazilian music.

Bluegrass:

Bluegrass is a genre that thrives on fast-paced, virtuosic playing. Guitar compositions in bluegrass frequently include tempo changes to emphasize transitions between verses, choruses, and instrumental breaks.

Example: *Foggy Mountain Breakdown* by Earl Scruggs and Lester Flatt is a bluegrass instrumental that features rapid tempo changes, highlighting the virtuosity of the guitar playing.

Classical Guitar Music:

Classical guitar compositions often involve tempo changes to emphasize different sections, convey emotional nuances, and showcase technical abilities. Composers use markings such as ritardando and accelerando to guide performers through these changes.

Example: *Asturias (Leyenda)* by Isaac Albéniz is a classical guitar piece that incorporates tempo changes to express the dramatic and passionate character of the Spanish *Leyenda*.

These examples illustrate how various genres use tempo changes as an integral part of their stylistic conventions. Whether it's for creating excitement, enhancing complexity, or conveying emotional depth, the strategic use of tempo changes contributes to the distinctiveness of each genre's guitar compositions.

METRONOME MARKINGS

Experiment with different metronome markings for various sections. A clear, quantifiable change in tempo can be effective in conveying the intended mood or atmosphere.

EXPERIMENTING WITH METRONOME MARKINGS

Experimenting with different metronome markings for various sections in a guitar composition is an effective way to explore rhythmic possibilities, create contrast, and enhance the overall musical expression. Metronome markings dictate the tempo of a piece, and varying them can influence the mood and character of different sections.

Identify Sections with Different Characteristics:
Start by identifying distinct sections within your composition. These sections might have different moods, dynamics, or rhythmic complexities.

Determine the Desired Mood for Each Section:
Consider the emotional and musical characteristics you want to convey in each section. For example, a faster tempo might convey excitement and energy, while a slower tempo might create a more contemplative or introspective mood.

Select Metronome Markings:
Choose metronome markings that align with the desired mood of each section. Metronome markings are typically given in beats per minute (BPM), and different

BPM values can significantly impact the feel of the music.

Experiment with Tempo Transitions:

Experiment with gradual or abrupt tempo transitions between sections. Gradual transitions can create a smooth and flowing feel, while abrupt changes can add contrast and surprise.

Use Different Note Values:

Experiment with metronome markings that emphasize different note values. For instance, a faster tempo with a higher BPM might make eighth notes feel more energetic, while a slower tempo might give more weight to quarter or half notes.

Explore Rubato and Tempo Flexibility:

Introduce rubato or tempo flexibility within sections to create expressive phrasing. While the metronome provides a steady beat, allowing for slight variations in timing can add a human touch to your playing.

Apply to Different Genres:

Experiment with metronome markings across various genres. Different styles of music may call for different tempos. For example, a blues section might benefit from a laid-back tempo, while a rock section may thrive with a more driving beat.

EXAMPLES

Classical Composition:

In a classical guitar composition, the allegro section might have a metronome marking of 120 BPM for a lively and upbeat feel. Transitioning to an andante section with a metronome marking of 80 BPM can create a contrasting, more relaxed mood.

Fingerstyle Acoustic Composition:

For a fingerstyle acoustic piece, a brisk tempo of 150 BPM could be used for a percussive and rhythmic section. Slowing down to 100 BPM for a melodic and introspective interlude can highlight the expressive qualities of the guitar.

Jazz Fusion Composition:

In a jazz fusion composition, a fusion groove section might benefit from a tempo of 160 BPM to convey energy. Transitioning to a ballad-like section at 80 BPM can create a distinct contrast, allowing for expressive improvisation.

Blues Composition:

In a blues composition, a shuffle section might thrive at a moderate tempo of 120 BPM, while a slow blues section could use a slower tempo of 70 BPM to enhance the soulful and emotive qualities.

Rock Guitar Solo:

In a rock guitar solo, a fast and virtuosic section might have a tempo of 160 BPM for intensity. Slowing down to 100 BPM for a melodic solo can allow for expressive bends and sustained notes.

Flamenco Composition:

A flamenco composition might feature a lively "bulería" section at 180 BPM for the fast footwork associated with this style. Transitioning to a slower "soleá" section at 100 BPM can showcase the guitarist's ability to convey emotion through phrasing.

Country Bluegrass Composition:

In a country bluegrass composition, a fast-paced picking section might use a tempo of 200 BPM for a lively feel. Slowing down to 120 BPM for a melodic breakdown can add variety and highlight the instrumental virtuosity.

Remember that these examples are just starting points, and the optimal metronome markings depend on the specific requirements of your composition and your artistic vision. Experimentation with different tempos and metronome markings will allow you to discover the most effective and expressive combinations for each section of your guitar composition.

TEMPO IS A TOOL

Remember that tempo changes are a tool to enhance musical expression, not a gimmick. Use them judiciously to serve the artistic goals of your composition.

USING TEMPO AS A TOOL, NOT A GIMMICK

While tempo changes can be a powerful tool for expressive and dynamic guitar composition, it's essential to recognize that using tempo as a gimmick can detract from the musical integrity and may not contribute positively to the overall listening experience.

Distracts from Musical Expression:
Using extreme or frequent tempo changes solely for the sake of novelty can distract the listener from the musical expression and emotional content of the composition. It may overshadow other essential elements such as melody, harmony, and dynamics.

Compromises Musical Coherence:
Excessive or erratic tempo changes can compromise the overall coherence of the composition. A lack of continuity in tempo may make it challenging for the listener to follow the musical narrative and connect with the piece on an emotional level.

May Seem Forced or Artificial:
When tempo changes are introduced arbitrarily, without a clear musical purpose, they may come across as forced or artificial. The transitions may lack a

genuine connection to the underlying musical content, leading to a disjointed listening experience.

Undermines the Role of Tempo in Musical Storytelling:

Tempo is a crucial element in musical storytelling, guiding the listener through different emotional landscapes. Using tempo as a gimmick can undermine its role in conveying subtlety, depth, and nuance within the composition.

Risk of Losing Audience Engagement:

Continuous and abrupt tempo changes may risk losing the engagement of the audience. If the listener perceives the tempo changes as arbitrary or disruptive, they may disengage from the musical experience.

Hinders the Development of Musical Themes:

Tempo changes should serve the purpose of enhancing the development of musical themes. If used as a gimmick, tempo shifts may overshadow the natural development of motifs, melodies, and harmonies, preventing the composition from reaching its full potential.

Overlooks Other Musical Elements:

Focusing excessively on tempo gimmicks may overshadow other essential elements of guitar composition, such as phrasing, articulation, and tonal color. A well-rounded composition should balance various musical aspects rather than relying solely on tempo changes.

GUIDELINES FOR PURPOSEFUL TEMPO CHANGES

While avoiding the use of tempo as a gimmick, it's important to recognize that purposeful tempo changes can greatly enhance a guitar composition when used thoughtfully. Here are some guidelines:

Serve the Musical Narrative:

Ensure that tempo changes serve the musical narrative and contribute meaningfully to the emotional expression of the composition.

Align with the Composer's Intentions:

Tempo changes should align with the composer's intentions and the overall mood or atmosphere they wish to create. Each shift should feel like a natural progression within the musical journey.

Provide Contrast and Variety:

Introduce tempo changes to provide contrast and variety within the composition. These changes can highlight different sections, create tension and release, and maintain listener interest.

Smooth Transitions:

Plan and execute tempo changes with smooth transitions. Gradual shifts or well-coordinated transitions ensure that the listener can seamlessly follow the changes without feeling disoriented.

Enhance Phrasing and Dynamics:

Use tempo changes to enhance phrasing and dynamics. Align shifts in tempo with expressive elements in the composition, such as crescendos, decrescendos, or notable melodic phrases.

Consider the Entire Ensemble:

If your composition involves multiple instruments, coordinate tempo changes across the ensemble to ensure a cohesive and unified performance.

Seek Balance and Subtlety:

Strive for a balanced and subtle use of tempo changes. Avoid extremes that might overshadow the overall musicality of the composition.

Remember, effective use of tempo in guitar composition requires thoughtful consideration and should contribute positively to the overall listening experience. When employed purposefully, tempo changes can elevate a composition, providing depth, emotion, and a compelling musical journey for the audience.

BALANCE IS THE KEY

Strike a balance between maintaining a consistent tempo for cohesiveness and introducing variety through well-timed changes. This balance ensures a compelling listening experience.

BALANCE CONSISTENCY WITH VARIETY

Striking a balance between maintaining a consistent tempo for cohesiveness and introducing well-timed changes in tempo is crucial for creating a dynamic and engaging guitar composition.

Establish a Solid Foundation:

Start your composition with a solid and consistent tempo. This serves as the foundation, providing a sense of stability and cohesion. Choose a tempo that aligns with the overall mood and character of your piece.

Identify Key Sections for Variation:

Identify specific sections or moments within your composition where introducing tempo changes would enhance musical expression or signify a shift in mood. These sections could include transitions between verses and choruses, key melodic phrases, or climactic moments.

Consider Emotional Context:

When contemplating tempo changes, consider the emotional context of your composition. Faster tempos might convey excitement and energy, while slower tempos can evoke introspection or contemplation.

Ensure that tempo variations align with the intended emotional impact.

Use Tempo Changes Purposefully:

Introduce tempo changes purposefully to serve the musical narrative. Whether accelerating for intensity or slowing down for emphasis, each change should contribute meaningfully to the overall flow and expression of your composition.

Employ Gradual Transitions:

Whenever possible, opt for gradual transitions between tempos. Gradual changes provide a smoother flow and are generally more pleasing to the listener. Experiment with ritardandos, accelerandos, or gradual shifts in time signatures for seamless transitions.

Coordinate with Dynamic Shifts:

Align tempo changes with dynamic shifts in your composition. For instance, consider increasing the tempo during a crescendo or slowing down during a diminuendo. Coordinating tempo and dynamics enhances the overall impact of these musical elements.

Experiment with Rubato:

Introduce tempo flexibility in expressive sections. This allows for nuanced phrasing and dynamic shaping without committing to a rigid tempo. Use rubato selectively to add expressiveness while maintaining an overall sense of tempo stability.

Connect Sections with Common Tempos:

Maintain a sense of connection between sections by using common tempos. While introducing variations, having shared tempos in certain sections can contribute to coherence and prevent the composition from feeling disjointed.

Explore Contrasting Rhythmic Elements:

Use tempo changes to explore contrasting rhythmic elements. For example, transitioning from a straight rhythm to a syncopated feel can add variety without necessarily changing the tempo. This approach keeps the listener engaged without drastic shifts.

Involve Other Instruments (if applicable):

If your composition involves other instruments, coordinate tempo changes across the ensemble. Ensure that all instruments contribute to a unified and coordinated approach to tempo variations.

Maintain Overall Flow:

Keep the overall flow of your composition in mind. While introducing variety, ensure that the tempo changes contribute positively to the natural progression of the music. Evaluate how each section leads into the next to maintain a cohesive musical journey.

Record and Listen Critically:

Record your composition and listen critically to the playback. Evaluate how well the balance between consistent tempo and well-timed changes enhances the overall listening experience. Make adjustments as needed to refine the balance.

Striking a balance between maintaining a consistent tempo and introducing well-timed changes requires careful consideration of the musical context and a keen awareness of the emotional narrative. By thoughtfully incorporating tempo variations, you can create a guitar composition that is both cohesive and dynamically engaging for the listener.

Remember, the key is to use tempo changes purposefully and sparingly, allowing them to serve specific musical goals rather than becoming a constant feature. This approach ensures that when tempo changes do occur, they have maximum impact, capturing the listener's attention and contributing to the overall artistry of your guitar composition.

The decision to include tempo changes in your guitar composition is a personal one, guided by the artistic vision you have for your music. Experimentation, thoughtful consideration, and a willingness to trust your intuition will guide you in determining where and how tempo changes can be most effective in conveying the emotions and narrative of your composition.

YOUR STRUCTURAL PLAN

Creating a structural plan for a guitar composition involves organizing the different sections of the piece.

OUTLINE FOR A STRUCTURAL PLAN

Below is a basic outline that you can use as a starting point. Adjustments can be made based on the style and complexity of your composition.

I. Introduction
A. Establish the key and mood
B. Introduce any recurring motifs or themes
C. Set the tone for the piece

II. Verse 1
A. Present the main melody or theme
B. Establish a harmonic progression
C. Introduce any rhythmic elements

III. Chorus
A. Build on the intensity or emotion
B. Introduce variations on the main theme
C. Consider a contrasting harmonic progression

IV. Verse 2
A. Develop the melody or introduce new elements
B. Experiment with different chord voicings
C. Provide continuity with the earlier sections

V. Bridge

A. Create a departure from the established themes

B. Experiment with a different key or mode

C. Build tension or anticipation

VI. Chorus 2

A. Return to a familiar theme with variations

B. Intensify the emotion or dynamics

C. Prepare for the final sections

VII. Solo or Interlude

A. Showcase technical proficiency or experimental elements

B. Connect the various sections

C. Transition smoothly to the final sections

VIII. Final Chorus or Climax

A. Build on the themes presented earlier

B. Increase intensity or dynamics

C. Conclude with a powerful statement

IX. Conclusion

A. Wind down the intensity

B. Recapitulate key motifs or themes

C. End with a conclusive chord or phrase

X. Outro

A. Provide a sense of closure

B. Fade out gradually or end decisively

XI. Optional Coda

A. Add a short concluding section for a final touch

B. Experiment with unexpected elements

This is a flexible outline and the structure may vary based on your creative preferences and the specific genre you're working in. Feel free to adapt and modify the plan to suit the unique character of your guitar composition.

YOUR TEMPO MAP

Creating a tempo map for your guitar composition involves planning and visualizing how the tempo changes throughout the piece. A tempo map serves as a roadmap, guiding the performance tempo at different sections of your composition.

Whether you're recording with other musicians or using a Digital Audio Workstation (DAW), a well-crafted tempo map helps ensure a cohesive and expressive performance.

CREATE YOUR TEMPO MAP

Here's a step-by-step guide on how to create a tempo map to guide you throughout your composition.

INITIAL DETERMINATIONS

Define Sections of Your Composition:

Identify Musical Phrases: Break down your composition into distinct musical phrases or sections. These could include verses, choruses, bridges, solos, or any part where the mood or intensity changes.

Determine the Initial Tempo:

Select a Starting Tempo: Decide on the initial tempo for your composition. This is often based on the mood and energy level of the opening section.

Example: Let's say your composition begins with a calm and reflective introduction, and you decide on a starting tempo of 80 beats per minute (BPM).

Mark Significant Tempo Changes:

Identify Key Moments: Highlight moments in your composition where a tempo change is necessary. This could be a transition to a new section, a change in mood, or a climactic moment.

Example: You've identified a section where the energy increases, leading to a chorus. You decide to raise the tempo to 100 BPM for the chorus.

Choose Transition Points:

Smooth Transitions: Determine where it's appropriate to transition between tempos. Plan for smooth transitions, avoiding abrupt changes that might disrupt the flow.

Example: To transition from the calm introduction to the energetic chorus, you decide to have a gradual accelerando over four bars.

Use Tempo Markings:

Marking in Notation: If your composition is written in standard notation, use tempo markings (e.g., ritardando, accelerando) to indicate where the tempo changes occur.

Example: In the notation, you write "rit." to indicate a gradual slowing down before a more contemplative section.

Consider Dynamic Changes:

Align with Dynamics: Coordinate tempo changes with dynamic shifts in your composition. For instance, if a section becomes louder and more intense, consider a corresponding increase in tempo.

Example: In a build-up towards a guitar solo, you decide to raise the tempo to 120 BPM, enhancing the excitement.

Experiment with Rubato:

Expressive Rubato: If your composition includes moments of rubato (flexible timing), use the tempo map to guide these expressive deviations from the steady tempo.

Example: During a melodic interlude, you plan for a rubato section with a gradual ritardando, allowing for expressive freedom.

Use Digital Audio Workstations (DAWs):

Set Markers: In your DAW, set markers at the beginning of each section and at key moments where tempo changes occur. This provides a visual guide for your tempo map.

Example: In your DAW timeline, you set markers at the start of the chorus and the beginning of the guitar solo section.

Implement Tempo Automation:

Draw Automation Curves: Use tempo automation features in your DAW to draw curves representing gradual tempo changes. This allows for precise control over the acceleration or deceleration.

Example: You draw a curve to smoothly increase the tempo from 80 BPM to 100 BPM over the course of four bars leading into the chorus.

Test and Refine:

Playthroughs: Test your composition by playing through it or listening to a MIDI mock-up. Pay attention to how the tempo changes feel in context.

Refinement: Make adjustments to the tempo map as needed. Fine-tune the timing of transitions and ensure that the overall pacing aligns with your artistic vision.

EXAMPLE TEMPO MAP

Section	Tempo (BPM)
Introduction	80
Transition	Gradual rit.
Chorus	100
Solo Build-up	Gradual acc.
Guitar Solo	120
Final Section	Rit.

In this example, the composition starts at 80 BPM with a calm introduction. A gradual ritardando leads to a transition, followed by an increase to 100 BPM for the chorus. The tempo then gradually accelerates during a solo build-up, reaching 120 BPM for the guitar solo. The composition concludes with a ritardando for the final section.

Creating a tempo map for your guitar composition involves thoughtful planning and consideration of the emotional and structural elements in your music.

YOUR RHYTHMIC DEVELOPMENT MAP

Rhythmic development is a crucial aspect of a guitar composition, adding dynamics and interest to the piece.

SECTION MAP

Here's an example section map for rhythmic development. Take it and make it your own for your guitar composition.

I. Introduction
A. Establish a simple rhythmic pattern to set the initial mood
B. Use basic strumming or picking techniques for a smooth introduction
C. Consider incorporating percussive elements to add texture

II. Verse 1
A. Maintain a steady rhythmic foundation with the established pattern
B. Experiment with variations in strumming or picking intensity
C. Introduce subtle syncopations to create rhythmic interest

III. Chorus
A. Increase strumming dynamics for a fuller sound
B. Explore more intricate picking patterns to enhance energy
C. Introduce a driving percussive element to emphasize the chorus

IV. Verse 2

A. Return to a variation of the rhythmic pattern from Verse 1

B. Experiment with muted strums or palm muting for contrast

C. Add rhythmic embellishments to build tension leading to the next section

V. Bridge

A. Break away from the established rhythmic pattern

B. Experiment with irregular time signatures for a unique feel

C. Use pauses and rests strategically to create tension and release

VI. Chorus 2

A. Revisit the rhythmic intensity of the first chorus

B. Develop variations in strumming or picking techniques

C. Introduce a rhythmic climax leading into the instrumental section

VII. Solo or Interlude

A. Allow for a change in rhythmic pace to highlight the solo

B. Use diverse rhythmic techniques such as arpeggios, legato, or staccato

C. Gradually build rhythmic intensity to transition back to the next section

VIII. Final Chorus or Climax

A. Increase strumming dynamics and rhythmic complexity

B. Experiment with accentuations and dynamic contrasts

C. Incorporate a rhythmic resolution for a powerful conclusion

IX. Conclusion

A. Gradually simplify the rhythmic pattern to wind down the piece

B. Use rhythmic patterns to create a sense of closure

C. End with a decisive final strum or picking pattern

X. Outro

A. Experiment with a subdued rhythmic pattern for a smooth exit

B. Gradually decrease the intensity of percussive elements

C. End with a final rhythmic statement to conclude the composition

This section map is just a starting point, and you can customize it based on the genre, style, and mood you want to convey in your guitar composition. Feel free to experiment with different rhythmic techniques and patterns to create a unique and engaging piece.

YOUR PHRASING MAP

Musical phrasing involves the shaping of musical ideas to create expressive and cohesive sections within a composition.

EXAMPLE PHRASING MAP

Here's an example phrasing map for a guitar composition. As usual, take this and make it your own for the development of your guitar composition.

I. Introduction
A. Establish a short, memorable melodic phrase
B. Keep the dynamics subdued to create anticipation
C. Repeat the initial phrase with slight variations

II. Verse 1
A. Introduce the main melodic theme for this section
B. Use legato phrasing for a smooth and flowing feel
C. Develop the theme with variations in pitch and rhythm

III. Chorus
A. Present a more uplifting and expansive melodic idea
B. Utilize dynamic phrasing to build intensity
C. Repeat the chorus theme with embellishments and octave jumps

IV. Verse 2
A. Return to a variation of the melodic theme from Verse 1

B. Experiment with staccato phrasing for contrast

C. Add slides or bends to enhance expressiveness

V. Bridge

A. Introduce a new, contrasting melodic idea

B. Use arpeggios or broken chords for an intricate feel

C. Build tension through ascending pitch and dynamic swells

VI. Chorus 2

A. Revisit the chorus theme with added embellishments

B. Experiment with phrasing variations like trills or grace notes

C. Increase intensity leading into the instrumental section

VII. Solo or Interlude

A. Showcase technical proficiency with rapid and fluid phrasing

B. Incorporate call-and-response phrasing with the backing instruments

C. Build towards a climax with ascending runs and wide intervals

VIII. Final Chorus or Climax

A. Present a powerful restatement of the chorus theme

B. Use sweeping arpeggios or tremolo picking for added drama

C. Conclude with a memorable melodic resolution

IX. Conclusion

A. Wind down the composition with a simple, emotive phrase

B. Use legato or vibrato for a gentle and reflective feel

C. Repeat a modified version of the introduction to create unity

X. Outro

A. Gradually decrease the intensity and volume

B. Experiment with a descending melodic phrase for closure

C. End with a final chord or harmonic for a conclusive finish

This phrasing map provides a framework for creating engaging and expressive musical sections. Feel free to adapt and modify it based on the specific style and emotion you want to convey in your guitar composition.

University Scholastic Press

CLOSING

Congratulations on completing your journey through *Rhythm Mastery for Guitarists: Unlocking Tempo and Timing Techniques For Guitar Composition.* You've delved into the intricate world of rhythm, explored its myriad facets, and equipped yourself with invaluable tools and insights to enhance your guitar compositions.

As you reach the conclusion of this book, take a moment to reflect on the knowledge you've gained and the skills you've honed. From mastering rhythmic patterns and timing to navigating tempo changes and incorporating dynamic elements, you've embarked on a transformative journey that has expanded your musical horizons.

But this is not the end of your rhythmic odyssey—it is only the beginning. The world of guitar composition is vast and boundless, offering endless opportunities for exploration and growth. As you continue on your musical path, remember to revisit the lessons and techniques presented in this book, allowing them to serve as a foundation upon which to build your creative endeavors.

I urge you to embrace the spirit of lifelong learning and discovery. Return to these pages whenever you seek guidance or inspiration, and let them fuel your passion for guitar composition. And remember, this book is just one entry point into the rich library of guitar composition resources offered by University Scholastic Press. Explore our other titles in the series to further expand your knowledge and skills.

Above all, stay true to your artistic vision and trust in your creative instincts. Let your passion for music guide you as you continue to craft compositions that resonate with meaning and emotion. Your journey as a guitarist is a deeply personal and rewarding one, and I am confident that you will continue to grow and evolve with each new composition you create.

Thank you for entrusting me as your guide on this rhythmic adventure. May your guitar compositions be filled with rhythm, passion, and boundless creativity.

Keep strumming!

THANK YOU

THANK YOU for purchasing *Rhythm Mastery for Guitarists: Unlocking Tempo and Timing Techniques For Guitar Composition* by University Scholastic Press. If you liked this book, please consider spreading your good word!

University Scholastic Press is an internationally renowned publisher and press, writing and producing textbooks, study guides, quote books, workbooks, cookbooks, journals, planners and creative nonfiction novels.

With offices in New York, London and Rome, University Scholastic Press is the trusted leader in producing and writing classic, bestselling books with an original, polished spin.

Other Musician Series Books By
University Scholastic Press:

A Guitarist's Grimoire: Unlocking the Secrets of
Creating A Musical Diary To Master Guitar Composition

Storytelling With Sound: Fundamentals of Creative
Guitar Composition

Musical Architecture Secrets: Structure Planning For
Guitar Composition

Strings Of Brilliance: Mastering Melody and
Harmony Development For Guitar Composition

Rhythm Mastery for Guitarists: Unlocking Tempo
and Timing Techniques For Guitar Composition

Index

University Scholastic Press

University Scholastic Press

Y

University Scholastic Press

www.ingramcontent.com/pod-product-compliance
Lightning Source LLC
Chambersburg PA
CBHW071303140726
47996CB00005B/1612